The DMT Diaries:
From Materialism to Modern Mysticism

Steven Turner

"We are not human beings having a spiritual experience; we are spiritual beings having a human experience."

- Pierre Teilhard de Chardin, **The Phenomenon of Man**

"If my eye is to discern colour, it must itself be free of colour. The eye with which I see God is the same with which God sees me. My eye and God's eye is the one eye, and one sight, and one *knowledge*, and one love."

- Meister Eckhart, **Sermons**

CONTENTS:

I 1
Inverted Inversions 2
The Relationship between Marx and Hegel

II 24
The Divine Comedy 25
The Hicks Factor

III 47
The Psychedelic Explorer 48
Terence McKenna: Poet of Entheogenic Ecstasy

IV 71
Realms of the Fantastic 72
The Phenomenology of DMT

V 95
Alien Dimensions 96
Science and the Multiverse

VI...119

Home of the Absolute *120*

5 MeO DMT and the Voyage to the Source

VII 143

The Totality of Mind *144*

The Akashic Field and the Pleroma

VIII...168

To Death and Beyond *169*

Near-Death Experience and the Multiverse

IX..192

Appendix:

Guy Debord and the Metaphysics of Marxism: *193*

An Obituary of Guy Debord

I

"Appearance is the process of arising into being and passing away again, a process that itself does not arise and does not pass away, but is *per se*, and constitutes reality and the life-movement of truth. In this way truth is the bacchanalian revel, where not a soul is sober; and because every member no sooner gets detached that it collapses straightway, the revel is just as much a state of transparent unbroken calm."

- G. W. F. Hegel, ***The Phenomenology of Mind***

Chapter 1

Inverted Inversions

The Relationship between Marx and Hegel

"I took to madness like a duck to water." wrote Christopher Gray as he embarked on a three year experiment with LSD towards the end of his life. This individual reengagement with a potent psychedelic was a dramatic personal shift, and catalysed a profound change within his beliefs towards the autumn years of his life. At the time he was still reeling from the breakdown of his relationship with his long term partner, and finding himself quite alone with feelings of depression and failure within the modern world. He felt as if he was perhaps a foolish romantic rebel, who had bet all on the heady idealism of his youth, and like most long-shot gambles, it had not come off. All that he seemed fated towards was the estrangement and social isolation of a man at odds with modern society, and facing his own mortality.

It was perhaps this sense of personal crisis and self-reflection that spurred him on to take one last gamble, in search of answers to his own life, and even the potential for some form of redemption. He then decided that the best avenue for adventure and enlightenment lay in the field of psychedelics. He was a brave man. He had not taken any form of hallucinogenic for many years, and the experiences he did have, he'd been either dismissive of as to their real social value, or at the other end of the spectrum, experiences which were truly terrifying. The fascinating journey he then embarked upon was then chronicled within his autobiographical book: ***The Acid Diaries, A Psychonaut's Guide to*** *the History and Use of LSD*. This book is now rated as a classic trip-report of one man's exploration into this powerful entheogen. What is also uplifting about this quest, is the therapeutic force it was to have in his life, and the valuable insights it was to give him for his own personal development. Though it must be said that these lessons were not always pretty, or even obvious to him at first. As with most entheogenic experience, it can be a very painful and often frightening encounter, when confronted with the psychological intensity of these spectacular visions:

"Everything was solidifying, as though something I had long understood intellectually could now be perceived directly: that, however distant in space or time, everything in the world was interconnected. Ultimately everything came down to being one thing, an incomprehensibly vast functioning whole, a single all-encompassing entity of which my body and mind were an integral part ... *and from which I as consciousness was shearing wildly apart ...*"

- Christopher Gray, **The Acid Diaries**

Christopher Gray was best known as one the key members of the British contingent of one of the most radical Marxist groups of the Twentieth Century - the *Situationist International*. Gray was one of the most influential figures of this group, which had for a short time constituted the English section of this small international organisation, until they (like most members) were eventually excluded. (In a note of irony, it was apparently their collaboration with an American colleague who was later charged with "mysticism," a grave charge from their continental comrades, in particular Debord and Vaneigem, that prompted this action). Gray was to go on to translate many of the key documents of this enigmatic group, and provide the first real introduction of this organisation's theories into the English language. He was to also provide a brief, though lucid commentary on the organisation's genesis, goals, and practical activities within the historical events of the Occupations Movement in France, culminating in the tumultuous year of 1968. This book was published in 1974 and was titled: ***Leaving the Twentieth Century, the Incomplete Work of the Situationist International.*** The book was to also feature the participation of such figures as Jamie Reid and Malcolm McLaren, and was later credited as a crucial influence on the birth and formation of the punk movement, their cultural attempt to express the situationists' ideas, and apply them to the subversion of the music industry:

"By the mid Sixties the situationist project had taken on its definitive form. The SI was to be a small, tightly knit group of revolutionaries devoted to forging a critique of *contemporary*, that is to say, consumer capitalism - and to publicising this critique by every form of scandal and agitation possible. All practical experiment with art went by the board. Everything depended on universal insurrection. Poetry could *only* be made by everyone."

- Christopher Gray, ***Leaving the Twentieth Century***

Gray had been hugely impressed with the sophistication of the situationists' critique of modern consumer capitalism, as well as its detailed analysis of the workers' movement, and the failure of the Marxist project of a classless society. The key text of the situationist movement was of course Guy Debord's book ***The Society of the Spectacle***, a book that one critic was to denote as the "***Das Kapital*** of this generation." This modest assessment was an opinion that Debord concurred with - he agreed that it was probably one of the most important books of the century. ***The Society of the Spectacle*** is a book of undeniable brilliance, which is not only a work of profound analysis, but also has an aesthetic literary quality which belies its origins within the artistic avant-garde. One of the key factors of this artistic beauty went unrecognised by some of its readership; in that the whole structure and dialectical fluidity of the book lay in its detournement of not only Marx's style and method of analysis, but equally its employment of the method of Hegel. Debord was not only highlighting his support for the "philosophical revisionists" Lukacs and Korsch, but also the very birthplace of Marxism within German idealism - namely the monumental philosophical system of Hegel. Marx had always claimed that his materialist conception of history was really an inverted form of Hegelian philosophy, that Hegel's core truth was simply "upside down." In an Afterword to the Second Edition of ***Capital*** he was to famously relate:

"My dialectic method is not only different from the Hegelian, but its direct opposite. To Hegel, the life-process of the human brain, *i.e.*, the process of thinking, which, under the name of "the Idea," he even transforms into an independent subject, is the demiurgos of the real world, and the real world is only the external, phenomenal form of "the Idea." With me, on the contrary, the ideal is nothing more than the material world reflected by the human mind, and translated into forms of thought. ... I therefore openly avowed myself the pupil of that mighty thinker, and even here and there, in the chapter on the theory of value, coquetted with the modes of expression peculiar to him. The mystification which dialectic suffers in Hegel's hands, by no means prevents him from being the first to present its general form of working in a comprehensive and conscious manner. With him it is standing on its head. It must be turned right side up again, if you would discover the rational kernel inside the mystical shell."

Debord also embraced this conception, and was very favourable to the theoretical works of the young Marx, his critique was that Marxism had become corrupted by Marx's economic analysis being transformed into a supposedly "pure" science of modes of production and class relations. Some socialists were to reduce this to a purely mechanistic sociological model which was crudely simplistic. Even Marx himself sardonically expressed his bafflement at some of his supporters misapplication of his theories, when he observed: "All I know is that I am not a Marxist." Both he and Engels were to emphasise this relationship towards the end of their lives, and they saw this problem as a generational thing, with many younger socialists being entirely ignorant of their philosophical mentor. Writing in the Twentieth century, after witnessing the sometimes horrific application of Marxist ideology in a number of different countries, Debord was to underscore this insight in a very stark manner:

"The determinist-scientific facet in Marx's thought was precisely the gap through which the process of "ideologization" penetrated, during his own lifetime, into the theoretical heritage left to the workers' movement. ... It is this mutilation, later accepted as definitive, which has constituted "Marxism."

- Guy Debord, *The Society of the Spectacle*

To truly understand Debord, and Marx, it is essential to have at least a working knowledge of Hegel, whose philosophical system had fallen into disrepute in the age of materialist science (from Darwin's theory of evolution, to Marx's own theory of the materialist conception of history), and was later scorned as simply the most elephantine edifice of rational mysticism ever created. This reputation was also exacerbated by the "Himalayan severity" of his prose, and the notorious difficulty of his work; which has made him one of the most despised intellectual figures to many a young student. It does seem, however, that he is making a modest comeback, as though Marx's theories seem to be increasingly discredited (not necessarily his critique of the functioning of capitalism, a more powerful global force than ever before, but more the functioning of so called communist societies and other variant socialist totalitarianisms), there seems to a genuine hunger for a different conception of history and man's place within it. Debord himself emphasised how the crude bastardisation of complex interpretations of Marx and Hegel had given birth to monsters:

"The *inversion* carried carried out by Marx to "recover through transfer" the thought of the bourgeois revolutions does not trivially consist of putting the materialist development of productive forces in the place of of the journey of the Hegelian Spirit moving towards its encounter with itself in time, its objectification being identical to its alienation, and its historical wounds leaving no scars. History become real no longer has an *end*."

- Guy Debord, ***The Society of the Spectacle***

The situationists often prided themselves on their megalomania, and in a way the most philosophical form of megalomania that has ever been created, was the gargantuan system of Hegel (at least according to Schopenhauer and Kierkegaard). Jung's assessment was equally withering: "The peculiar, high-flown language Hegel uses bears out this view - it is reminiscent of the language of schizophrenics, who use terrific spellbinding words to reduce the transcendent to subjective form..." As Hegel's was a metaphysical corpus that incorporated every philosophical school of thought before it, and presented itself as the final fruition of the human intellect comprehending itself, and the universe in systematic form. In Bakunin's candid assessment of his and Marx's theoretical influences he was to write:

"Unless you had lived in those times, you will never understand how powerful the fascination of this philosophical system was in the 1830s and 1840s. It was believed that the eternally sought Absolute had finally been found and understood, and that it could be bought wholesale or retail in Berlin."

- Michael Bakunin, ***Statism and Anarchy***

Hegel presented his system as not only a new philosophical doctrine, but essentially the culmination and completion of philosophy. It thereby superseded all previous schools of thought, by incorporating and transcending them, like a circle that completes itself. History is therefore seen as a progressive force in which God, or "the Absolute," rises to full self-consciousness of itself as the ultimate cosmic form of self-knowledge. This is a process that is only accomplished with Hegel's own comprehensive system of absolute idealism. The centrepiece of his system is ***The Phenomenology of Mind*** - the voyage of mind is traced from sense-certainty through various phases of developing self-consciousness, each drama a necessary stage to its final destination of "Absolute Knowledge." God is not viewed as an external force outside the universe, but rather an immanent process within it, which can only now review and comprehend its own dialectical self-development. No book has ever come to such a dramatic conclusion, to end philosophical history as it reveals itself to be this end, and to portray all world history as a theodicy which mankind undergoes to complete this divine self-realisation. A system that seemed to also include every field of human knowledge within it - including art, science, philosophy and religion. As Hegel was not only a philosophical genius, he was also a man of vast learning in every domain he studied. As the elderly Engels noted:

"... logic, philosophy of nature, philosophy of mind, and the latter in its turn worked out in its separate, historical sub-divisions, philosophy of history, of right, of religion, history of philosophy, aesthetics, etc - in all these different historical fields Hegel laboured to discover and demonstrate the main thread of development. As he was not only a creative genius but also a man of encyclopedic erudition, he played an epoch-making role in every sphere."

- Frederick Engels, ***Ludwig Feuerbach and the End of Classical German Philosophy***

The main reason Hegel is being rediscovered and his work is being re-assessed is the whole historicist thrust of his philosophy, which regards the fluid notion of truth within its evolutionary historical context. Very few people today, however, see his system as a genuine ontological proof of absolute idealism, and are at times embarrassed by the religious conclusions he draws. Very few scientists would take Hegel's religious views seriously, as God has been thoroughly banished from nearly all forms of materialist science. Science is at war with most forms of religious doctrine, in particular the frightening rise of fundamentalism within all the major monotheistic creeds; which hold the view that the literal interpretations of their holy texts trump any new scientific discovery. The scientific world is understandably scornful of these developments, and fearful that this fanaticism would lead us back to the dark ages of pre-enlightenment thinking, where faith subverted reason, and undermined the whole edifice of scientific thought. Some scientists are so militantly atheistic, that religion is now viewed not just as quaintly superstitious, but as a form of mental illness. Looking at the evidence of human conflict around the globe at the moment, it is easy to understand their concern.

But just as it seemed that as our increasingly sophisticated knowledge of the universe would completely banish religion from all our investigations, in some fields rationalist science has uncovered strange anomalies and paradoxes that have again forced us to question all our underlying core assumptions. It will be in these areas that this book will attempt to shine a light, and hopefully to approach these subjects open-mindedly. As some of the evidence of what we uncover may force us to question the very fabric of our concept of reality. This book cannot provide scientific *proof* of any of the subjects which are raised, and in some fields, believes this may *forever* be the case; all it can offer is individual testimony, scientific speculation, and some of the most staggering theories offered by some of the world's brightest minds.

To return briefly to Hegel again, he is often regarded as the apex of thought from the golden age of German Enlightenment philosophy. He is sometimes regarded as the true successor of Kant, that other giant of the German intellect. While this is a fair assessment, for Kant was to have a huge influence on his developing thought, the other philosophy which was to also have a significant impact on him was the elegant and enigmatic pantheism of Spinoza. Spinoza's work was to play a vital role in forming the colossal edifice of Hegel's system of rational mysticism. Other schools of thought were also to have a contributory role within his intellectual development - Jakob Boehme, Schelling, Leibnitz, and Fichte were all key important influences, but surely it was Spinoza's rational pantheism that was the pivotal force which steered him towards his own logical form of pantheism "or panentheism" as some critics would later designate it:

"God is the indwelling and not the transient cause of all things. All things that are, are in God. Besides God there can be no substance, that is, nothing in itself external to God. ... The human mind has ideas from which it perceives itself and its own body and external bodies as exactly existing; therefore it has an adequate knowledge of the eternal and infinite essence of God."

- Baruch Spinoza, ***Ethics***

Spinoza is sometimes called the "Jesus of philosophy" not just for his innate integrity and gentle spirit, but mainly for the unwarranted persecution that he was subjected to during his own lifetime. He was from a traditional Jewish background, but was excommunicated when, because of his razor sharp intellect, he was to question the religious texts of his culture. There was even an assassination attempt upon him when he refused to have his silence bought. He was then forced to live quietly in exile, first in Amsterdam, and then at the Hague. There he continued to write and refine his beliefs, and made his modest income by grinding lenses, as these were at the time the cutting edge technology of the day. Most of his work was never published until after his death, as his religious heresy was still considered a scandal in the age in which he lived.

The ideas that Spinoza developed possess a peculiar beauty that many can find almost incomprehensible. In that the logic that they follow develops in a formal mathematical manner, which is almost like literary Euclidian geometry. Each axiom seems to be build upon the premise of its predecessor. A style which the modern mind can find very perplexing. It is as if faith is being constructed as a branch of logic, to which many of religious faith would find the very antithesis of belief:

"Individual things are nothing but modifications of the attributes of God, or modes by which the attributes of God are expressed in a fixed and definite manner."

- Baruch Spinoza, ***Ethics***

The core of Spinoza's philosophy was that Nature and God were essentially the same thing. God was not an entity existing outside the universe, guiding and intervening within it, but rather the totality of everything. He believed that the inconsistencies in the Bible were evidence of this lack of understanding of God's true nature. These ideas may not seem controversial in these modern times, but they were considered scandalous in Spinoza's era, and many great thinkers such as Leibnitz hid his influence on them, for fear of damaging their reputation.

Spinoza's philosophy had certain characteristics that were also shared with the German mystic - and humble shoe-maker Jakob Boehme. Like Spinoza, Boehme's beliefs aroused condemnation from the orthodox church, and he was threatened with exile if he allowed his writings to be published and circulated amongst the public. Boehme abstained from writing for many years, and it was only his small circle of friends and admirers who persuaded him not to neglect his talent. Boehme's philosophy differed from Spinoza's pantheism in that it centred around the idea of redemption, and in particular the Fall from Grace that man had endured. Boehme, who claimed that his insights were gained during moments of mystical insight, stressed that it was through man that God had alienated himself: by the cleaving of man from his original state of innocence. This was to achieve a new level of perfection and self-awareness - through the overcoming of this necessary and transformative suffering. This was the truth that was contained in the parable of the exclusion of man from the Garden of Eden. Suffering was a necessary stage of self-consciousness, in its voyage to a higher form of perfection, and was an essential aspect of man's free-will. These ideas were to have a significant impact on

Hegel's system, which was entirely grounded in this process of alienation, and the overcoming of this alienation in order to achieve a higher-form. This was a form of mysticism that included pain within its path of transcendence:

"When you art gone forth wholly from the creature [human], and have become nothing to all that is nature and creature, then you are in that eternal one, which is God himself, and then you will perceive and feel the highest virtue of love. Also, that I said whoever finds it finds nothing and all things, that is also true, for he finds a supernatural, supersensual Abyss, having no ground, where there is no place to live in, and he finds also nothing that is like it, and therefore may be compared to nothing, for it is deeper than anything, and is as nothing to all things, for it is not comprehensible, and because it is nothing, it is free from all things, and it is that only Good, which a man cannot express or utter what it is."

- Jakob Boehme, *The Way to Christ*

All three of the major monotheistic religions (namely Judaism, Christianity, and Islam), contained within them mystical schools of thought that developed from more ancient branches of esoteric wisdom. These influences often predated these world religions (such as Zoroastrianism and Hereticism), and often contained a much more sophisticated and complex account of creation and sacred knowledge than the more literal and dogmatic accounts of the church orthodoxies. These schools of thought (such as Gnosticism, Kabbalah and Sufism), shared many of the same ideas and beliefs as each other. They could even be said to share together more of the same commonalities of thought than with their own parent religions. The churches reaction to them (in particular Gnosticism in the case of the Cathars), has sometimes been not only persecution, but also genocide. The case of the Cathars in southern France during the early Medieval period was even a source of fascination for the young Guy Debord, while he was a member of the Lettrist International (a precursor of the Situationist

International). The Cathars' theology was a combination of Paulician, Manichean as well as Gnosticism, and was to provoke theological as well as political disputes with the Catholic church: which were to culminate in the notorious *Albigensian Crusade*, and the virtual annihilation of this now obscure sect. These beliefs have still managed to endure though, even if they have mutated slightly with the passage of time. In his fascinating book on the religious and philosophical traditions connected to the pineal gland within history, Anthony Peake observed:

"These traditions, Sufism, kabbalah and Christian Gnosticism, have been attacked many times as being heretical by their mother religions, but still they survived. Is it possible that this survival is because they present a model of the universe that seems inherently logical and instinctively true to many people? This is why many esoteric schools have taken the Gnostic philosophy and applied it to create new models of understanding. These schools are part of the hidden history of the modern world."

- Anthony Peake, *The Infinite Mindfield*

Different interpretations of these beliefs will be examined in more detail in the light of developments within a number of specialist fields. These controversial scientific subjects did not exist until fairly recently in our history, and even now are considered to be in their comparative infancy. We are certainly witnessing huge breakthroughs in these subjects within our own lifetime though. The data, and interpretation of this data, is generating huge excitement within the small communities that are studying these disparate though interrelated phenomena. Four of the key areas we will need to investigate will be the *near-death experience, modern cosmology, quantum physics* and *psychedelics*, particularly the *tryptamine* family. And of all the alkaloid tryptamines, two of the most fascinating compounds known to brain chemistry must be N,N-DMT, and its closely related cousin, 5 MeO DMT. Both of these chemicals are endogenous (produced naturally) by the human body, but they are also probably the two most powerful psychedelics known to man. They are both prevalent throughout nature; in a variety of plants and animals, but the answer as to specifically what their real function is in consciousness remains contentious. In fact, they are one of the most intriguing mysteries facing mankind today. To quote one of DMT's most vocal and charismatic supporters - the endearing Terence McKenna:

"Here is the tremendum barely to be told, an epiphany beyond our wildest dreams. Here is the realm of that which is stranger than we *can* suppose. Here is the mystery, alive, unscathed, still as new for us as when our ancestors lived it fifteen thousand summers ago. ... DMT as we have discussed earlier, occurs as a part of ordinary human neurometabolism and is the most powerful of the naturally occurring indole hallucinogens. The extraordinary ease with which DMT utterly destroys all boundaries and conveys one into an impossible-to-anticipate and compellingly Other dimension is one of the miracles of life itself. And this first miracle is followed by a second: the utter ease and simplicity with which enzyme systems in the human brain recognise the DMT molecule at the synapses."

- Terence McKenna, **Food of the Gods**

The philosophical implications of the tryptamine 5 MeO DMT are even more astonishing if the reported phenomenology of its subjective trip-reports are found to be authentic. These accounts will always be difficult (if not impossible) to verify in a strictly scientific manner, but if the case studies of medically authorised N,N-DMT (the Strassman studies) are anything to go by, then we may have to reassess all our current foundations of materialist science. What is important, is to study these phenomena with as rigorous a scientific method as possible, in order to best illuminate and decipher what this information is truly telling us. For if the classic trip-reports of N,N-DMT consistently and repeatedly produce accounts of experiences within different dimensions to our own: the phenomenology of 5 MeO DMT consistently give rise to a very different spiritual dimension. The most authoritative accounts of these experiences all imply an infinite field of consciousness - the divine metaphysical source of all reality:

"This suggests that all conscious beings are analogous to waves rising up from an ocean of collective singularity. The ocean is a single entity but each wave swells up for a short amount of time and then disappears back into the singularity. Each wave contains water molecules, physical manifestations of the underlying ocean that exist within the wave itself. The essence of life that is analogous to the water molecules in the waves is DNA."

- Anthony Peake, ***The Infinite Mindfield***

The reason we are exploring these different models of reality, is that they are a touchstone to the philosophical dispute that is as old as human culture itself. Throughout history, the two major antagonistic philosophical schools of thought have been idealism and materialism. Both have diametrically opposed opinions as to what the fundamental source of reality is. Throughout the history of classical philosophy, different metaphysical systems have been devised to explain the world of thought and its relationship to the external world, and throughout history different philosophies have overthrown each other in search of the solution to this enigmatic riddle. At present, the paradigm of rational materialism holds sway within most fields of science, and idealism holds court in a minority of scientists and in peripheral way. This may be something of an over simplification, as many of the greatest scientists in world history (Einstein, Eddington, Newton to name but a few) had mystical inclinations; but the fundamental sentiment within the core of science is unquestionably materialist. This orthodoxy is not blanket, or even claims it has found solutions to all the physical mysteries of the universe, but it does believe it possesses both the tools and method through which to solve these puzzles. The limitations of this scientific quest are however posed by one the most celebrated physicists of our time:

"Even if there is only one unified theory, it is just a set of rules and equations. What is it that breathes fire into the equations and makes a universe for them to describe? The usual approach of science of constructing a mathematical model cannot answer the questions of why there should be a universe for the model to describe."

- Stephen W. Hawking, *A Brief History of Time*

One of the most paradoxical developments within this debate is surely one of the most successful sciences of the Twentieth and Twenty-First centuries - *quantum mechanics*. The success of our understanding of this field has underpinned most of the revolutionary technology of our modern age. It will almost certainly be the source of much of our future visionary technology too (with applications such as nanotechnology and quantum computing). This will undoubtedly have a profound effect on all our daily lives. One of the key paradoxes of quantum mechanics though - is that despite it giving birth to some our most accurate statistical predictions so far recorded (to a degree many other sciences are envious of), the more mysterious and perplexing are its implications for the nature of reality itself. In fact, to those few geniuses who understand its workings in a depth greater than anybody else, the more baffling and incomprehensible are its findings. Many of the founding fathers of this science were themselves so astonished by the theories mechanisms, that they too were driven to forms of Eastern mysticism in search of explanations. Quantum mechanics has invariably inspired many a science-fiction writer as well, because the search for a coherent scientific model of its nature can lead to some of the most extraordinary and bizarre conclusions that the human imagination can produce.

One of the most famous quantum physics experiments is known as the double slit experiment, and was to discern whether a photon of light was in fact a wave or a particle (as it was known that it could behave like either in different experiments). When a single particle of light was fired through a double slit screen, its impact was recorded on a light sensitive film on the other side. Even though only *one* photon was fired individually, the image that was produced showed the signal pattern of interference (these interference patterns clearly showed that the photon had acted as a *wave* and must have travelled through both slits *at the same time*), thereby proving that light was in fact a wave. However, when recording devices were added to the experiment to *measure* which slit the photon travelled through, the results were completely different. When the photon was actually *observed,* the interference patterns disappeared, and the photon, behaved as a *single particle*. This experiment has now been run numerous times, and has become a central feature of quantum mechanics, and is known as the collapsing of the wave function. It essentially implies that the act of observation *determines* whether a photon behaves as a wave or a particle. This would also seem to imply that in truth it is *consciousness* that determines the nature of reality at the quantum level, the act of *observation* that creates the external world. The full implications of these results are hotly contested, and many theoretical models have been devised to try to make sense of these results. Although by no means is this question fully resolved, it does indeed seem to give valuable scientific support to the idealist camp, as to the primacy of mind and matter - and the evidence drawn from one of the most successful branches of materialist science so far developed.

Another of quantum physics enigmatic anomalies is known as "*quantum entanglement*" which has yet again been verified by the most sophisticated and rigorous experimentation. The main problem though, is that it appears to break the speed of light boundary which is at the core of relativity theory (Einstein himself called it "spooky action at a distance"), and is still inexplicable within our current scientific understanding. It essentially implies that any two "entangled" particles that have had physical contact are in symbiotic relationship, in that what you do to one immediately affects the other - regardless of the distance between them. The speed of light condition which is so essential to relativity states that nothing, including any form of information, can break this parameter. Yet once again, this has been scientifically verified by the most advanced technological experimentation available: that a form of "quantum symmetry" occurs. It seems to suggest that the mystics insight that everything is somehow connected to everything else in the universe has real scientific validity. Somehow the universe is connected in such a complex and holistic way that it is in some sense a singularity that only functions as a whole.

This was an idea that was comprehensively developed by one of the most interesting quantum physicists of the Twentieth century - *David Bohm*. Though born American, he was from a Jewish background, and because of the political climate, he lived a significant portion of his adult life in England (Bohm like a lot of intellectuals from his generation were sympathetic to Marxism: he was to show courage and integrity by never implicating any of his associates during the McCarthy era, preferring exile to betrayal). Later in his life, his "mystical" interests catalysed friendships with Krishnamurti and the Dalai Lama, who referred to Bohm as his "personal physicist." Bohm believed that mind and matter co-exist in different dimensions that unfolded and enfolded each other (this he referred to as the *Implicate and Explicate Order*). Reality was in fact an infinitely multidimensional and multilayered totality - an unbroken wholeness, and what we perceive as the world is only a fragment of this "holomovement." It is also believed that Hegel's formidable tome, the **Science of Logic** was a seminal influence on his most famous work: **Wholeness and the Implicate Order**. The entire universe, with all its different fields and particles was in fact a single totality and unbroken whole, and what we perceive as autonomous units, are in fact only aspects of an underlying unified activity. Bohm was to also collaborate with the acclaimed neuroscientist Karl Pribram, who had been working independently on a theory that the brain stored information *holographically*, and realised that Bohm was himself developing similar ideas, in which the universe itself functioned in very much the same way: as a hologram. They both, from different fields, arrived at complementary conclusions. That the part - like fractals, also contained the whole, and belonged to a deeper underlying unity. Bohm also believed that it was our flawed perception of reality that had underpinned our fragmented mindset, and prevented us from discerning the true nature of the world:

"The best image of process is perhaps that of the flowing stream, whose substance is never the same. On this stream, one may see an ever-changing pattern of vortices, ripples, waves, splashes, etc. which evidently have no independent existence as such. Rather, they are abstracted from the flowing movement, arising and vanishing in the total process of the flow."

- David Bohm, **Wholeness and the Implicate Order**

"You cannot step twice into the same river; for fresh waters are ever flowing upon you."

- Heraclitus

What has this got to do with Marx and Hegel I guess you are wondering? When Marx and Engels were formulating their theories of the materialist conception of history, this was a period of science when materialism was on the ascendency. Darwin's theory of evolution was rightly hailed as one of the greatest scientific achievements within human history. And natural selection was acknowledged as the biological mechanism and motor underlying the creation of all species. All of the physical sciences were flourishing, and bit by bit nature was slowly giving up her secrets - through "experiment and industry" to use an expression of Engels. Idealist doctrines were often seen as rooted in ill conceived, and out-moded metaphysical speculation, a product of religious backwardness, and thereby destined for the dustbin of history. Science was seen to be uprooting these archaic superstitions, and repositioning mankind's proper place in the material universe. No longer based on untestable speculation and hypotheses, but on testable, repeatable scientific experiment. The human race was now viewed as simply the genetic spawn of random natural selection, and man was simply an animal like any other, but simply more intellectually advanced than its primate cousins. Both Marx and Darwin had seemingly dealt the deathblow to all forms of philosophical idealism, and had convincingly put materialism back on the throne. There it has essentially remained since. Both Marx and Engels though, were well acquainted with current scientific developments (Engels was a keen student of most areas of natural history). They would therefore have taken a keen interest in the cutting-edge discoveries of their day, and would unquestionably have taken an interest in the astonishing results and speculation within the new science of quantum physics, had it existed in their day. What impact it would have made on their doctrines can now only be a subject of pure speculation:

"Consciousness can never be anything else than conscious existence, and the existence of men in their actual life-process. If in all ideology men and their circumstances appear upside-down as in a *camera obscura*, this phenomenon arises just as much from their historical life-process as the inversion of objects on the retina does from the physical life-process."

- Karl Marx and Frederick Engels, ***The German Ideology***

Yet again the rules of the game are apparently changing, and the debate between idealism and materialism has been reignited. Both camps are equally passionate about their belief system, and each camp would fault the other with the charge of blinkered vision, and corrupting the method of science through obvious impartiality. The materialist camp asserts that matter is the true fabric of the universe, and consciousness is simply an epiphenomenon created by the chemical communication within brain chemistry. The idealists stress the observer paradox of quantum physics, and challenge materialism to find evidence of how any process of chemical combinations can produce the phenomenon of self-awareness. This issue is often known as the "hard problem" and is rooted in the mystery of how consciousness and matter interact or are just different aspects of each other. This debate lies at the heart of this book, for the question of what exactly *consciousness is*, is the most fundamental question of all. And it is the investigation of consciousness within the context of *altered states* that may paradoxically prove the key to unlocking this mystery.

When Christopher Gray began his experimentation with LSD towards the end of his life (at this point he was probably already suffering from the lung cancer that would eventually claim him), the conclusions he would come to would surprise if not shock him - probably him more than most people. This is a man who was an authentic situationist, and former colleague of Guy Debord, and was often scathing of all organised religions - or certainly their exploitative uses. Despite his once hardline atheism (he had though spent many years in India exploring a more spiritual outlook, but had become disillusioned with this quest), the experiences he was to encounter with the high-end acid doses are certainly not uncommon. These transpersonal epiphanies are a characteristic of most tryptamine entheogens. Whether these boundary dissolving experiences reflect a true insight into the real nature of reality, or simply a distorted hallucination triggered by intoxicated brain chemistry is as contentious now as ever. To the individual though, the reality of the experience is undeniable:

"As I write this, true recall of what I felt, the existential suchness of it has gone. But like the no-boundary states that summer, what I do remember perfectly is its overwhelming self-evidence. *I was everything*. It was as simple as that. Nor was it something I had just become, I always had been everything. What was really difficult to understand was how I could ever have thought I was anything else."

- Christopher Gray, ***The Acid Diaries***

So it would seem that yet again the controversy between these two incredibly influential world-historical thinkers (Hegel and Marx) is far from over - and in a way personify the very essence of this scientific debate - as they also represent two of the last comprehensive philosophical "system builders" with diametrically opposed perspectives. When Marx thought he had solved the "riddle of history" he presented a pretty convincing case - whether you agree with all his political doctrines of not (the basic anthropological model of how the economic base determines the cultural and political superstructure of all human societies, is still a powerful metaphor for explaining history). However, recent developments in science have thrown these ideas yet again into question, and history may yet prove that it is Hegel who will slyly have the last laugh. It would truly be one of the great ironies of history, if it was Marx himself who ends up being inverted and be placed "right-side up," to reflect the true model of reality. This reality may transpire to be a thousand times more complex and multidimensional than we had possibly anticipated. In the same way that cosmology has over the last century been astonished by its discovery of the true scale of the universe: which we now know is on a scale which would be considered unfathomable not many generations ago (and that is before we factor in the debate about the *multiverse* and the almost infinite possibilities it raises with different dimensions, and possibly a *metaverse*). The question of intelligent design is also being raised in a serious fashion, as to the incredible fine-tuning necessary for a universe that is hospitable for life. The solution to these questions are as daunting now as they have been to any other era. Maybe our time is not so very different after all. It is rumoured that shortly before his death, the old Hegel pronounced this observation on his philosophy: "Only one man has understood me and even he has not."

The basic questions that he struggled with, and the metaphysical complexities he wrestled with are still with us, only now in slightly different philosophical and scientific forms. Throughout the centuries visionaries have tried to articulate similar conceptions, and though they may have been separated by time, place, and language, their message can sometimes still be strikingly in accord:

"Spirit is the only Reality. It is the inner being of the world, that which essentially is, and is *per se*; it assumes objective, determinate form, and it enters into relations with itself - it is externality (otherness), and exists for itself; yet in this determination, and in its otherness, it is still one with itself - it is self contained and self complete, in itself and for itself at once. ... it is Substance spiritual. It has to become self-contained *for itself*, on its own account; it must get knowledge of spirit, and it must get consciousness of itself as spirit."

- G.W.F. Hegel, ***The Phenomenology of Mind***

" ... all matter is merely energy condensed to a slow vibration. That we are all one consciousness experiencing itself subjectively. There is no such thing as death, life is only a dream, and we're the imagination of ourselves."

The man who spoke those words was not a cloistered scholar, academic, or professional philosopher. He was an authentically spiritual man who hated the hypocrisy and corruption of most organised religions. He would use his corrosive wit and acidic humour to unmask the exploitation of the credulous and gullible by odious fraudsters who choose to manipulate religious and spiritual sentiment for political and financial gain. He was in fact an American stand-up comedian, who blazed a trail of righteous anger through England and America during the Eighties and Nineties, and achieved more in his short life than many in their dotage. He was also one of the funniest guys who ever performed. He was *Bill Hicks*.

II

"If we consider Spirit in this aspect - regarding its changes not merely as rejuvenescent transitions, *i.e.* returns to the same form, but rather as manipulations of itself, by which it multiplies the material for future endeavours - we see it exerting itself in a variety of modes and directions; developing its powers and gratifying its desires in a variety which is inexhaustible; because every one of its creations, in which it has already found gratification, meets it anew as material, and is a new stimulus to plastic activity. The abstract conception of mere change gives place to the thought of Spirit manifesting, developing, and perfecting its powers in every direction which its manifold nature can follow."

- G. W. F. Hegel, *The Philosophy of History*

Chapter 2

The Divine Comedy

The Hicks Factor

"Good evening, brothers and sisters, friends and neighbours, vibrations in the mind of the one true God whose name is love." So opened Bill Hicks's first ever filmed half-an-hour special, recorded at the Old Vic in Chicago, and was titled ***One Night Stand.*** This opening line might have sounded whimsical or even sarcastic to some of the audience of an "alternative" comic, especially one with as dangerous and edgy a reputation as Bill Hicks - but he was in fact being totally serious. He may have attacked the types of religious dogma and hypocrisy that characterised certain forms of *Christian fundamentalism* (or at least the laughable inanity of some of its theology), but at heart he was a very spiritual guy. In fact, it was probably this intellectual sensitivity that fueled his anger at organised religion in the first place.

Bill (full name William Melvin Hicks "Thanks Dad." his dry observation) was born in Valdosta, Georgia on December 16th, 1961 but moved around frequently in his early years, and was finally settled in Houston, Texas when he was seven years old. Here he was raised by his loving middle-class Southern Baptist parents, Jim and Mary, along with his two older siblings, Lynn and Steve. Bill would often mock his parents for their conservative and conventional religious beliefs, but obviously always held a deep affection for them, even if they found his rebellious comedy almost incomprehensible throughout the majority of his years. They were to be all drawn back together towards the end of his life, as Bill wanted to face his final months of terminal illness with them all together as a family, to reconnect, and also "to close the circle."

Growing up in Houston, he was fortunate enough to find a small circle of friends that would remain important to him throughout his life. Friends like Kevin Booth, Dwight Slade, and David Johndrow who though sometimes separated geographically, because of the meandering life of the touring comic, still remained close, and often just a phone call away. Bill was always a loyal and supportive friend, and it was this generosity of spirit that often endeared him to those closest to him. Fame never altered Bill's relationship to those who were a part of his close circle - it was no doubt galvanised by the *camaraderie* of sharing a similar outlook to life, and which had distinguished them from most of their contemporaries (who were no doubt a constant source of amusement to them). Though Bill was popular amongst his friends, he would still consider himself as something of an outsider, as the ambience of conformist, suburban, middle America must have seemed suffocating and somewhat banal to such an intelligent and questioning a personality as Bill's. Fortunately he was blessed with a creative talent for channeling this source of frustration - a razor sharp sense of humour. And this is why it would always be fun to hang around with him. The seeds of Bill's sophisticated brand of dark humour were first sown by observing this underbelly of the American Dream, and the shallow small-mindedness that seemed to constitute much of suburban American life. Here it seemed free-thinking was not nurtured and encouraged, but rather seen as a mental deficiency or social problem. At one point his parents became so concerned with his rebellious attitude, they sent him to see a psychoanalyst, after listening to his perspective, he was advised: "You can continue if you want to, but it's them, not you."

Bill would first start to gain recognition as a performer at the *Comedy Workshop* in Houston, at this point he was still a teenager, but it was even then obvious to all of his contemporaries that he possessed a rare talent, and could hold court in a club of adults totally unphased. A circle of comics had been drawn together there whose material was distinctly more cerebral and edgy than was common in the comedy explosion that took place in the Eighties: when a public thirst for humour hit its peak and comedy clubs all over the country sprang up to cater for this demand. The Houston entourage were to famously christen themselves the *Texas Outlaw Comics* - as they envisioned themselves as comedy mavericks, that were willing to push boundaries and break rules to pursue a higher vision of comedy; which not only entertained, but also had a social message. They were prepared to push their audiences expectations as well, with material that would not only make them laugh - but also push them to think for themselves:

"The fact that we live in a world where John Lennon was murdered, yet Barry Manilow continues to put out fucking albums. Goddam it. If you're gonna kill somebody have some fucking taste. I'll drive you to Kenny Roger's house, all right? Get in the car I know where Wham! lives."

- Bill Hicks, **Dangerous**

The lineage of "great" alternative comics is always a hotly disputed topic, and individual preferences are always subjective - but there is no doubt that Lenny Bruce will probably be the first to be seen as this pioneer. This mantle could also be a burden though, as he was a man who was willing to challenge his audience's beliefs and prejudices, and take comedy into areas that before him were socially taboo - and this was to incur a very high personal cost. Lenny Bruce certainly deserved this reputation, and the legal persecution that he then encountered not only confirmed his perspectives, but also took a toll on his personality and comedy. The intolerable pressures that he was subjected to, were to exacerbate his drug problems, and send him on a downward spiral that was to lead to his premature death, through overdose. It is no doubt a cliche that the life of a comic is a dangerous one, because of the nature of the lifestyle and environment make it a minefield for the temptations of both drink and drugs; but this cliche is also very real. Not to mention the idiosyncratic psychological factors that go into making a professional comic in the first place.

In the history of comedy though, it is surely recognised that it was *Richard Pryor* who marked a watershed, turning comedy from a form of entertainment into an a fully fledged art-form. His two greatest performances: **Richard Pryor Live in Concert** and **Live on the Sunset Strip**, are still seen as the benchmarks that showcase some of the greatest comedy ever performed, but equally a continuing inspiration for countless comedians as an almost unattainable ideal. The genius of Pryor was not only his incredible visual dexterity and timing, but his ability to turn his follies and addictions into a source humour itself. His often brutal candour and honesty made him a legend in the comedy world, simply for speaking in such an open way about the demons that haunted him. This was surely a turning point in the history of comedy - not just the racial taboos and observations that formed the central core of his perspective and act, but also sex, death, and chemical addictions which are universal problems across the globe. His audience loved him for the mocking way he was to illuminate all human frailties, with an honesty and intimacy that cut right to the bone. Richard Pryor will assuredly be recognised as the man who not only changed comedy - but the man who changed *what comedy could be*.

As important as Bruce and Pryor's influence were on Bill, they was not alone. One of the most neglected influences on Bill Hicks was probably *Sam Kinison*. In England the roles between Bill and Sam Kinison in terms of public popularity are probably reversed, and it is Hicks who is famous and Kinison who has little recognition. In America though, after years of comparative obscurity (although often a vital force in the *Texas Comedy Outlaws*, and a performing companion of Bill), Sam Kinison became a big hit after appearing on a Rodney Dangerfield comedy special, and was suddenly catapulted to national fame. After this he could fill arenas, and cultivated the persona of a "comedy rock star," with all the inflated vices that went with that title. Sam had a reputation for the enjoyment of sex, drugs, and alcohol, every bit as disreputable as his musical equivalents. What was most interesting about Sam, was not only his anguished trademark scream (though this was certainly an important aspect of it), but the fact that he was himself once a genuine "hell-fire" Pentecostal preacher (a vocation shared by most of his family), who had turned sides, and gone over to a very different style of preaching. He had chosen comedy over religion after many years within the ministry, and after the collapse of his marriage. He had also become disillusioned with the church, but had an insider's knowledge of not only its canon and theology, but also its methods and techniques. Bill's fascination with Sam was not only his angry confrontational style, which gave him a license to say what he wanted, regardless of his crowd's sensibilities, but to also deliver his message with power and intensity - without any pretence of getting the audience to like him. Sometimes you could *shock an audience into listening*. This was a revelation to the young Hicks, and certainly had an impact on his subsequent development. Sam's passion and moral indignation, especially at the greed, hypocrisy, and corruption that he saw within the *Televangelism movement*, which had become huge during the Eighties - and was to become rocked by a number of scandals that in themselves, simply went beyond comedy. Bill would often joke that his real competition was not other comics, but those other theatrical and truly hilarious performers - Christian Televangelists. Bill was to take his assault and satire of this commercialisation of Christianity further, and challenge the very core and ideology of the religion's doctrines:

"Such a weird belief. Lots of Christians wear crosses around their necks. You think that when Jesus comes back he's gonna want to see a cross man? ... You know it's kinda like going up to Jackie Onassis with a rifle pendant on, you know. "Thinking of John, Jackie. We love him. Just trying to keep that memory alive, baby."

- Bill Hicks, ***Revelations***

Late in the Eighties Bill was to have to undergo a personal transformation himself. During his teenage years, Bill had eschewed drink, drugs and smoking. In fact, he used to mock anyone who used to dabble in any of these potentially destructive pleasures. However, when he did start to experiment, often in a bid to push his performance to further extremes, he was typically pulled to gargantuan excess himself. With his frustration at his audiences appreciation of him growing, and his own lack of wider success, this was to fuel his own path of extreme hedonism and potential self-destruction. Like Bruce, Pryor, and Kinison before him, he was inevitably drawn into a lifestyle of reliance and addiction, as extreme performing personalities often are. As alcohol and cocaine became increasing prerequisites for his act, this would not only fuel the intensity of his angry performances, but to also alienate his audiences still further. As his dependence became more cripplingly acute, he was to show another great strength of character - by confronting and triumphing over his addictions - and still manage to maintain the brilliance of his performances. In fact, his shows got sharper, smarter, better.

This was obviously not achieved overnight - it was an incredibly painful period for him, one that took many months to complete, but when he did set his mind on sobriety, he never relapsed. He would never use alcohol or hard drugs like cocaine again. The only exception to this rule were *psychedelics*, in particular *magic mushrooms*, which he did not consider to be a physically harmful or addictive drug, but rather an *entheogen*, that acted as a spiritual *part* of his recovery. This distinguishment between harmful and destructive drugs (irrelevant of their legality), was also to become an important part of his worldview, as well as a celebrated part of his act. Bill never became a moraliser about his drink and drug experiences, itself a feat; but chose to instead highlight the fallacies and corrupt logic of the government's supposed "War on Drugs." Bill would skillfully demonstrate that this was not only a complex problem, one with many subtle grey areas within it, but also one often based on ignorance as well as vested interests:

"I think it's interesting the two drugs that are legal, alcohol and cigarettes, two drugs that do absolutely *nothing* for you at all, are legal, and the drugs that might open your mind up to the fact of how badly you are being *fucked every day of your life*? Those drugs are against the law. He-he, coincidence? See I'm glad mushrooms are against the law, 'cause I took 'em once and do you know what happened to me? I laid in a field of green grass for four hours going: "My God! I love *everything.*" Yeah, now, if that isn't a hazard to our country ... how are we gonna justify arms dealing if we know we're all *one*?!"

- Bill Hicks, **Shock and Awe**

Bill became reinvigorated by this change in his lifestyle, and this drove him to concentrate on cultivating his message with added momentum. This was to lead to an acceleration of his creative output, and inspire him to find a wider audience through the performances that he could now finally get produced, and distributed in media form. Though he remained something of an underground figure, he was finally able to reach an audience that was not only appreciative of his comedy, but also identified with the message he was trying to articulate. Finally it seemed that he was beginning to get the recognition he deserved. It was at this point in his life he was to play a pivotal comedy festival in Montreal, and his outstanding performance there was to attract the attention of the *Channel Four* crew from the UK, which was there to cover the event. They were so impressed, that Bill became the sole focus of their attention: this became the material that formed his first full televised show that was aired on British television, and almost overnight turned him into a cult comedy figure within the UK. This show was titled **Relentless,** and was essentially the big break Bill had longed for, and was most importantly, achieved on his terms. In the UK he was never forced to censor his material in the way he had to for American corporate television, in particular the *Letterman* show, which he was a frequent guest on. Since this, and his classic **Revelations** performance, with which he was to follow up **Relentless** with (which was broadcast almost in its entirety on *Channel Four),* his comedy reputation has not only endured: it has even increased over the years. Bill is now considered as one of the true comedy greats (at least in the UK), despite the relatively few filmed comedy performances he was able complete within his short lifetime. His appeal lay in the candid manner he was to explore all the contradictions and paradoxes that made modern life, and tackle thorny issues with his own unique and edifying perspective:

"They're putting the cart before the horse on this pornography issue. *Playboy* doesn't create sexual thoughts. There are sexual thoughts, and *therefore* there is *Playboy*. Don't you see? I know that these seem deep philosophical questions: "What came first, the hard-on or the Madonna video?" and "If a hard-on falls in the forest, do you go blind?" and "What goes an atheist scream when they come?"

- Bill Hicks, **Relentless**

Hicks has been described by one reviewer as the "Guy Debord of comedy," and there is an element of truth to this observation, even if it is unlikely that either was aware of each other, or would even embrace this recognition, as they were from two very different worlds. In terms of the content of their worldviews though, there is definitely a lot of common ground. Bill's targets were not only organised religion, but capitalism, consumerism, the mass-media "Lucifer's dream box," militarism and politics. Bill's comedy not only developed and matured throughout the years, but also took on an increasingly sophisticated critique of modern society in all its cultural forms. The topics he discussed such as the Kennedy assassination, the first Gulf War, the Los Angeles race riots were all hot topics - which he was to forensically dissect with the skill or a surgeon, and allow the audience to question their own beliefs, and contemplate the veracity of the information it was receiving. All this, and also be hugely, unthinkably funny too:

"You know we armed Iraq. I wondered about that too, you know. During the Persian Gulf War those intelligence reports would come out: "Iraq: incredible weapons - incredible weapons." How do you know that? "Uh well ... we looked at the receipts."

- Bill Hicks, ***Revelations***

One of Bill's favourite topics was also the role of the media within popular culture, and his diagnosis was that it served and functioned as an anesthetic to critical thinking. That its role was a premeditated distraction, to keep a population hypnotised with a plethora of empty and meaningless trivia. The growing power of this media industry reflected its colonisation of most of people's leisure-time, and dominated the whole development of a society's consciousness. Bill was often savage at what he saw as the degrading and cheapening of a culture's mental evolution, by the quality of its entertainment. He believed the media industry, like any other successful business organisation, also had vested interests at stake, and profited in keeping a population culturally retarded. His disgust would also extend to the audiences who revelled in these inane delights:

" ... go back to bed, America: your government has figured out how it all transpired. Go back to bed America: your government is in control again. Here, here's *American Gladiators*. Watch this! Shut up! Go back to bed America: here's *American Gladiators*. Here's fifty-six channels of it. Watch these pituary retards bang their fuckin' skulls together and congratulate you on living in the Land of Freedom. Here you go, America. You are free - to do as we tell you."

- Bill Hicks, ***Revelations***

Bill had finally found a platform for his voice, and an audience that not only approved of his message, but also embraced him as a personality. When Bill returned to America he would joke that he seemed to be following the route of one of his musical heroes - the great Jimi Hendrix, and be discovered in the UK before gaining recognition in his homeland. Even Bill's friends were shocked when they were to see his televised shows broadcast on UK primetime, and marvel that "Bill is like a rock star over there." But just when it seemed that all of Bill's hopes and ambitions were about to be realised, fate was to deliver one of its cruelest jokes, in a manner that is still almost beyond comprehension. For Bill was at the peak of his creative game - and his lifestyle was probably cleaner than any other comic around (he had even quit smoking for a time, his last remaining vice). He was not only honing his beliefs, but also exploring new mediums to extend his message. He was even starting to combine his music (Bill was an accomplished guitar player), with his recorded stand-up shows, an experiment in combining all his talents in a single art-form:

"People say to me: "Quit talking about Kennedy, man. Let it go. It was a long time ago. Just forget about it." All right then don't bring up *Jesus to me*. I mean as long as we're talking shelf-life here. "You know, Bill, Jesus died for you ..." Yeah it was a long time ago. Forget about it. How about this: get Pilate to release the fuckin' files. Quit washing your hands, Pilate, and release the files. Who else was on that grassy Golgotha that day? Oh yeah, the three Roman peasants in $100 sandals. Yeah, right?"

- Bill Hicks, ***Arizona Bay***

He was definitely at the height of his powers when he was devastatingly diagnosed with pancreatic cancer, a condition he hid from nearly everyone around him. He not only bravely undertook medical treatment for the disease on the road, but also continued his punishing tour routine, and continued to develop projects for the future (if anything he increased his workload). He was set to write a book, and was being commissioned by *Channel Four* in England to create his own television show titled: **Counts of the Netherworld**. The format was to feature each week a different topic, for him and his comedy colleague Fallon Woodland, to investigate and explore. It is very telling that the only two guests that were top of their lists, and perfect candidates for enlightening conversation, were the famous linguist and anarchist: Noam Chomsky (Bill was extremely impressed with Chomsky's voluminous critiques of the function of the mass-media in modern democracies), and the cult psychedelic raconteur *Terence McKenna*. McKenna's fame had been steadily growing throughout the late Eighties, as was his literary output as well. His growing demand on the public speaking circuit continued to climb; as an interested audience became more and more intrigued by his theories. The reason for Bill's initial interest in Terence's work was his own exploration and experience with psychedelics, in particular, psilocybin magic mushrooms, a subject that Terence was something of an authority on. Bill's own psychedelic experiences, and the insights they were to initiate, were to become not only central to his beliefs - but also an important part of his act as well. On his **Relentless** titled CD he was to expand on what he felt it was that magic mushrooms had taught him:

"Your mind completely opens up to the true nature of existence, which is that we are not bodies, that we are pure, loving spirit created by God. That God is love and there is nothing but love, being all-encompassing has no opposite. You are completely forgiven on all things, there's nothing you've ever done that has ever swayed God's pure and unconditional love for you. And you realise that eternity and peace and heaven is our inheritance, all of us are going to make it there."

These epiphanies he felt were some authentic form of divine communication from a higher state of consciousness. This was a direct and unmediated revelation, which completely bypassed all orthodox religions: "unnecessary middlemen" according to Bill, and was accessible to anyone who was prepared to undergo its rigours. Bill not only considered these experiences as sacred, but also achieved through the ingestion of a completely untampered product of Mother Nature. Bill's experiences were nearly always pursued using the same set and setting. He had no sympathy for people who took hallucinogens, and then went to theme-parks, and had bad, frightening trips. Anyone who was that stupid in their understanding of what this sacred ritual involved, he felt deserved everything they got. He was equally scathing of people who leapt out of buildings after taking LSD:

"Always the same LSD story; you've all seen it: "Young man on acid, thought he could fly, jumped out of a building. What a tragedy." What a dick, fuck him! He's an idiot. If he thought he could fly, why didn't he take off from the ground first? Check it out. You don't see *ducks* lining up to catch elevators to fly south. They fly from the ground you moron. Quit ruining it for everybody. He's a moron, he's dead - *good*. We lost a moron - fucking celebrate."

- Bill Hicks, from **Love All the People**

It is well known amongst psychedelic explorers, that set and setting are of crucial importance, and often *the* most important factor in how you will experience these altered forms of consciousness. Anybody who is foolish enough not to make serious preparations for their state of mind, or external environment, is often inviting disaster, or at least a very bumpy ride. Bill and his friends would usually pursue this experience in a familiar setting - and what they considered to be the optimal environmental conditions for a transcendent state. They would trip together, so they could be supportive of each other, and they would usually do it in a quiet, beautiful, and secluded part of nature. This was often on a ranch which was owned by one of their families, and in which they knew they would not be disturbed. Bill would often remark on this in his act, and advise his audience about what the quality of these experiences were: "They are sacred. Go to nature." Within this context, their trips could then unfold in a setting which would be as harmonious as possible, and unclouded by any outside distractions. It does not guarantee a beautiful experience - but it does increase their odds. Bill would, however, recall how one time when he was not so cautious in his preparations, and ended up in a situation he would relate to as a lot worse than any "nightmare drunk" scenario you could possibly contemplate:

"Not all drugs are good, now. OK? Some of 'em are great. Just gotta know your way round 'em is all. Yeah, I've had good times on drugs. I've had bad times on drugs, too. I mean, shit, look at this haircut. There are dangers. ... You know. You just gotta be careful. We got pulled over tripping on acid one night, pulled over by the cops. Don't recommend it."

- Bill Hicks, ***Revelations***

He then hilariously recounts how being interrogated by the police is not the ideal situation to be in, when you are tripping on a potent, mind-altering and illegal hallucinogenic. A fact I'm sure many in the audience could well appreciate. These substances should always be treated with caution and respect - and when abused, or taken for simple "entertainment" purposes, may give the experiencer a lot more than they bargained, and certainly wished for. This should not detract from the *potential* of entheogens though, because when employed intelligently, and with the correct motivation, can facilitate some of the most beautiful and meaningful experiences that the human mind can comprehend. The psychedelics that Bill had utilised and promoted are known not to be physically harmful or addictive. In fact medical science (before they were made illegal by the sweeping drug laws that were draconianly introduced in the late Sixties and early Seventies) has even employed them as therapeutic tools that can often help cure, and overcome, self-destructive habits and addictions. The fact that they did become abused, and scandalised by a generation, was as much to do with the politics and social transformations of that era, as it does with the potential benefits and productive uses that they are capable of. One of the most important elements of the psychedelic experience for Bill was its potential to help re-appraise the whole way you looked at life, and possibly decondition you from a lot of thoughts that you had simply subconsciously absorbed and accepted:

"Cos all your beliefs, they're just that. They're nothing, they're how you were taught and raised. That doesn't make 'em real. That's why I always recommend a psychedelic experience, cos it does make you realise everything you learned is in fact learned and not necessarily true."

- Bill Hicks, from ***Love All the People***

Probably the most important "psychedelic" experience Bill would ever have, would be his planned celebration of the *Harmonic Convergence* in 1987, a time of planetary alignment that was thought to have some equal spiritual significance. Bill and his friends prepared for the event in a disciplined, and quite meticulous manner, and believed that it would probably be their greatest chance to have a transcendent experience of real significance. They changed their diet, and undertook periods of yoga and meditation, in order to prepare their bodies for what could possibly be one the best opportunities for a breakthrough entheogenic experience of almost cosmic proportions. These expectations were incredibly not only realised, but even surpassed. The story is best understood from the account of probably Bill's best friend, and the only person he was to directly share this experience with. It is worth quoting in great detail, to really understand the impact it had on him:

"We took five grams. Five grams of dried mushrooms is a lot. If you wanted to punch a hole through the fabric of space-time, five grams is good. But don't try it yourself at home or at my families ranch or any place unless you are ready and willing to cross the threshold. ... We sat back down and the next thing we knew, we opened our eyes and we share this UFO experience. From a descriptive standpoint, it's almost ridiculous to talk about as visually it did seem like something from a bad science-fiction movie. ... The inside of the ship was like a conch shell. I walked down a circular ramp through a hallway of light and headed to a circle of light. The beings, they were glowing. Again, describing how things looked starts to sound absurd, but they looked like Mr Burns from *The Simpsons*, specifically in the episode where he emerges from the forest looking like an alien. His eyes dilated and his body glowing green - the aliens were lustrous like that.

Bill and I were both in the ship. He was asking questions like: "Why are you here? Why is this happening?" I remember coming out with explanations of time travel and a firm belief that the barriers to time travel and communication were all inside our mind. Basically, anything was possible.

At the time I was thinking that my head conjured up this image just for me to see, then Bill indicated to me he had seen and experienced the exact same thing. ... After that we realised we were able to communicate telepathically. It was way beyond just being able to make people laugh when tripping, like the experiences Bill first had when he took mushrooms and went on stage to do comedy, the time when he thought he was reading the audience's collective mind.

This was very specific. For the first time ever, Bill and I were able to say things and hear each other back, able to ask questions and get answers. We had a perfectly normal conversation without either one of us opening our mouth. We were in perfect sync. It was like a miracle. We communicated like this for a while, neither of us saying anything. ...

It went from the two of us being able to communicate with each other, to us being dialed into a network where now we were openly communicating with hundreds, thousands, maybe millions of minds at the same time. There was something identifiable in it, like we could trace where their voices were coming from and who they were. Everybody was sharing this moment because they wanted to. And it was unbelievable. We just laid on the floor and stayed tapped into whatever we were tapped into. ... But the spaceship, that was the most important thing that ever happened to Bill. He saw the "source of light that exists in all of us." Later he said, "God, I hope that was just the first of many things just like that." ... Bill believed he had direct communication with another intelligent life form that was trying to show him what the future could be like. And the future was all about love, light and acceptance."

- Kevin Booth, ***Bill Hicks, Agent of Evolution***

When Bill would reference his UFO experience, much of the audience was unsure how seriously to take him. He was obviously a very intelligent and well educated individual, so even some of his friends were embarrassed by this apparently "flakey" side to his character, and question the credibility of such a story. A lot of people were simply confused: was it a joke, was it a metaphor, or was it just Bill's concept for some kind of Cosmic form of Global Enlightenment? Most of his fans were happy to give him the benefit of the doubt, and simply adopt whichever interpretation best suited their own individual worldviews. When a guy was this funny, and so right about so many other subjects, most of his admirers were simply happy to maintain a very loose view on such a controversial subject. Bill, however, was very explicit about his convictions, and often conveyed them in a very direct manner, even if the audience would usually interpret these stories as simply part of a wider punchline. When hallucinogenic drugs are involved, most people would account for the experience as simply an intoxicated imagination:

"I have seen UFO's split the sky like a sheet, but I have never looked at an egg and thought it was a fuckin' brain. I have had seven balls of light come off of a UFO, lead me on to their ship, explain to me telepathically that we are all one and there's no such thing as death. *But ... I've never looked at an egg and thought it was a fuckin' brain. Now ... maybe I wasn't getting good shit, but ahh ... "*

- Bill Hicks, ***One Night Stand***

Throughout the years Bill's opinions did evolve as to what the wider implications were for the role of natural psychedelics in the development of the human mind. Under the influence of Terence McKenna, he would begin to question what possible role natural hallucinogens could have in fact played in human evolution. This concept is known as the "stoned ape theory," and was given great support by the publication of McKenna's famous book: ***Food of the Gods***. The central idea was that in our prehistory, huge environmental changes forced our species to descend from the trees, and scavenge for food on the great pastures of the open African savannah. There they would encounter the possible food source of psilocybin magic mushrooms, which grow naturally on cattle dung. This potential food group would give mankind its first real encounter with these altered states of consciousness. It was conceived that it was these states that could have triggered the "brain explosion" that our species has undergone in our comparatively recent history (at least in terms of evolution). This brain explosion is unprecedented in any other species - and the theory points to natural hallucinogens as the possible catalyst. The theory conjectures that these altered states were possibly the very birthplace of language and conceptual thinking - as well as possibly our first religious experiences too. Although this theory has never been scientifically proved, it does offer a tantalising explanation of the development of human language and culture. As well as forcing us to reassess our whole relationship with natural psychedelics, and rethink their potentially colossal significance within human history itself. These ideas fascinated Bill and he was to incorporate them into his act:

"I believe that God left certain drugs growing naturally upon our planet to help speed up and facilitate our evolution. OK, not the most popular idea ever expressed. Either that or you're real high and agreeing with me in the only way you can right now. I forgot the code - is it two blinks "yes," one blink "no"? Do you think magic mushrooms growing atop cowshit was an accident? Where do you think the phrase, "that's good shit" came from? Why do you think Hindus think cows are holy? Holy shit! Why do I think McDonald's is the Anti-Christ? That's God's little accelerator pad for our evolution. Let's think about this, man.

For billions of years - sorry, fundamentalists - we were nothing but apes. (*makes chimp noises*) Probably to stupid to catch a cow .... [chimp investigates, then consumes magic mushrooms] (*chimp noises and mime ending in laughter*). "I think we can go to the moon." (*hums theme tune from **2001: A Space Odyssey***). That is exactly how it fucking happened."

- Bill Hicks, **Revelations**

Bill was fascinated by this idea that psychedelics were not only an important tool for unlocking the doorway to higher realms, where mankind could access states of consciousness that were beyond our normal senses. He was equally intrigued by the possibility that our very evolution could have been shaped by our collective use of these sacred plants and fungi. It is currently being investigated by some committed researchers as to what part ancient mushroom cults played in the formation of a number of world religions. Mushroom cults are known to have existed all across the world, as well existing in a number of different cultures. They are also known to have predated all the major monotheistic religions, and could certainly have had an influence on their early formation. Bill would no doubt have been interested in these controversial subjects, because he often equated psychedelic experiences with *mystical* revelations, and would certainly class these products of nature as *entheogens:* "generating the divine within." They are viewed as tools, or a technology, that we know has been utilised for thousands of years throughout mankind's history, as a way of accessing information and knowledge that is usually outside, or beyond the normal range of human perception. To Bill, our true purpose was to evolve, and develop our minds, and to move our ideas further towards this goal of a more transcendent form of knowledge:

"Folks, it's time to evolve ideas. You know, evolution did not end with us growing thumbs. You do know that, right? Didn't end there. We're at the point now where we're going to have to evolve ideas. The reason the world's so fucked up is we're undergoing evolution. And the reason our institutions, our traditional religions are all crumbling is because they're no longer relevant. ... So it's time to create a *new* philosophy and perhaps even a new religion, you see. And that's OK, cos that's our right, cos we are free children of God with minds who can imagine anything, and *that's kind of our role.*"

- Bill Hicks, from ***Love All the People***

To Bill there was no conflict in his philosophy of exposing social injustices, and denouncing inequalities, and at the same time developing his aspiration for a higher form of consciousness. Like the French intellectual Guy Debord, the struggle for social justice, was a corollary to a higher form of human society. One connection between Guy Debord and Bill Hicks which has apparently been missed by many of their readers and audience - is their mutual appreciation of *John Steinbeck*. Debord would always consider himself very much a classicist. The whole body of his work is deeply embedded in this literary tradition and canon, and he made few acknowledgments to more modern writers. However, in his autobiographical work ***Panegyric,*** he would reference one of Steinbeck's lesser known novel: ***Cannery Row***. This is one of Steinbeck's lesser famous books, but which a small minority might consider as their personal favourite. ***Cannery Row*** is enthused with a warmth and humour that is unrivalled in any of his other works, and possesses a charm that could melt even the hardest hearts. The fact that all the main characters in the story are heavy drinkers, is no doubt an attraction to Debord, but so is the obvious bohemian ethos that runs through the whole book (with characters like Henri the painter, who "threw himself so violently into movements that he had very little time left for painting of any kind" must have knowingly amused Debord), and is also bursting with brilliant and endearing observations. The book is a real pleasure to read, and re-read. In a filmed interview, Kevin Booth disclosed that Bill kept a tattered old suitcase, in which he kept all his prized possessions, the things that he privately treasured. In that suitcase was a copy of one of Steinbeck's greatest works: ***The Grapes of Wrath***. This was a book which had a great impact on the young Hicks, and a story that he was intimately familiar with (Bill would often joke about the Joad family in his act). When he was dying, he would formulate his departing message to the world, and one which reflected beautifully on the quality of his character:

"I left in love, in laughter, and in truth and wherever truth, love and laughter abide, I am there in spirit."

- Bill Hicks, from ***Love All the People***

Kevin Booth had recognised that what Bill had done was to paraphrase the famous speech from Tom Joad, which had captured the essence of the book, and its committed confrontation of social injustice. He had simply reworked the message to communicate his own philosophy of life, and his own spiritual cause:

"Wherever they's a fight so hungry people can eat, I'll be there. Wherever they's a cop beatin' up a guy, I'll be there."

- John Steinbeck, ***The Grapes of Wrath***

It is a strong testament to Bill's philosophy and perspective, that he could compose such a beautiful epitaph under such cruel conditions, at the end of his far too short life, at the age of thirty-two. His message still remained one of hope and happiness, despite the terrible circumstances of his illness. This is why many of his fans were to find exquisite pathos in the concluding speech of probably his most famous and celebrated show. This could then function as a balm to all those who privately mourned his individual loss:

"The world is like a ride in an amusement park. And when you choose to go on it, you think that it's real because that's how powerful our minds are. And the ride goes up and down and round and round. It has thrills and chills, and it's very brightly coloured, and it's very loud and fun, for a while. Some people have been on the ride for a long time, and they begin to question - is this real, or is this just a ride? And other people have remembered, and they come back to us. They say, "Hey! Don't worry, don't be afraid, ever, because, this is just a ride." And we … *kill* those people. Ha ha ha. "Shut him up! We have a lot invested in this ride. SHUT HIM UP! Look at my furrows of worry. Look at my big bank account and my family. This just has to be real." It's just a ride. But we always kill those good guys who try and tell us that, you ever notice that? And let the demons run amok. But it doesn't matter *because*: it's just a ride. And we can change it any time we want. It's only a choice. No effort, no work, no job, no savings and money. A choice, right now, between fear and love.

The eyes of fear want you to put bigger locks on your door, buy guns, close yourself off. The eyes of love, instead, see all of us as one. Here's what we can do to change the world, right now, to a better ride. Take all the money that we spend on weapons and defence each year, and instead spend it feeding, and clothing and educating the poor of the world, which it would many times over, not one human being excluded, and we could explore space, together, both inner and outer, for ever, in peace. Thank you very much, you've been great."

- Bill Hicks, **Revelations**

In concluding this chapter on Bill, it may be helpful to recognise how deep the influence of the enigmatic psychedelic explorer Terence McKenna was on him. He, like Bill, was also travelling across the country, as well as abroad, in order to communicate with his growing body of fans, and spread his message at the same time. He too was an incredible public performer, and could spellbind an audience with his incredible tales. If Bill was the comic, then Terence was surely the storyteller. He also possessed a wit and command of language which even rivalled Bill's. It is a great sadness that these two equally inspirational individuals never found the opportunity to meet, as the chances are they would have become friends. He is the man that we will now turn our attention to:

"Bill often referenced Terence McKenna from the stage when he talked about the UFO experience. McKenna was once described as the Magellan of psychedelic head space. A true child of the Sixties, after graduating from the University of California at Berkeley he spent time studying native Amazon plant life and hallucinogens, particularly as they related to the local shamanic traditions.

McKenna thought that tryptamine based hallucinogens, such as those found in magic mushrooms, were a vehicle for communicating with other life forms across the universe. He was particularly fascinated by a pronounced consistency of experience amongst people ingesting large dosages - he referred to these greater than 3.5 grams, as "heroic" (Bill often alluded to this term on stage, and often exceeded that amount when taking mushrooms). People taking such large doses were, with noticeable frequency, reporting that they were going to a place, a realm he described as inhabited by entities he termed "self-transforming machine elves."

The way these entities were perceived was based on the hallucinogen and the context in which it was taken. For example, McKenna found that DMT, once extracted from plants, purified and smoked, invariably resulted in the user having a UFO abduction experience.

So when Bill talked about mushrooms and evolving and UFOs he wasn't joking."

- Kevin Booth, **Bill Hicks, Agent of Evolution**

III

"Finite things are; but their relations to themselves is this, that, being negative, they are self-related, and in this self-relation send themselves on beyond themselves and their being. They are, but the truth of their being is their end. The finite does not only change, like Something in general, but it perishes; and its perishing is not merely contingent, so that it could be without perishing. It is rather the very being of finite things, that they contain the very seeds of their perishing as their own Being-in-Self, and the hour of their birth is the hour of their death."

- G. W. F. Hegel, *Science of Logic*

Chapter 3

The Psychedelic Explorer

Terence McKenna: Poet of Entheogenic Ecstasy

"The harmine molecule, which is structured like a little bell, gives a bell-like chiming and buzzing sound. If we come in on it right and cancel it there is neural DNA active in the brain, the electrical configuration of harmine is enough like the molecular configuration of adenine, one of the bases in DNA, that it will replace it. It will bond through into the chain. and when it is bonded in, its ring will be activated. It is the same size as adenine, but it's a little more complicated. It has a free resonance ring." Dennis paused and then gathered his thoughts to continue.

"Now the normal ESR of harmine is a simple signal, but the electron spin configuration of DNA is very, very complicated. It is a broad band. When the harmine goes in there it will cease to broadcast its own resonation because it will have become very tightly bonded into the structure of the macro-molecule. It will instead begin to broadcast the ESR resonation of the DNA. That's it. If you have followed it this far, the rest is easy. DNA is what you are. The physical form is just a lot of juicy macro-physical crystals caused by gene expression, you know, the result of enzymes set in motion and coded by DNA. Neural DNA is known to be non-metabolizing. It does not go away. The meat on your body comes and goes every few years. Your skeleton is not the same one you had five years ago, but neural DNA is an exception. It is there for all time. You come into the world with it. It records and is an antenna for memory. Not only our personal memory, but any entity or organism which has DNA in it; there is a way to find a connection to it. This is how we open a passage to the Divine Imagination, this is how William Blake understood Redemption. This is now within reach.

This is how it's done. You put a radio into the DNA and this ESR resonation will begin to flood your system because the bond will be permanent; there will be no way to disrupt it. It will tell you everything - everything that can be known in the world of space and time because it contains your own and everyone else's records. We are all connected through this magical substance, which is what makes life possible and which causes it to take on its myriad forms. All DNA is the same. It is the settings that are different; you get butterflies, mastodons, or human beings, depending on the settings."

- Terence McKenna, ***True Hallucinations***

This is Terence's description of his brother Dennis's elaboration of what would become known as the "experiment at La Chorrera," and this event was to cast a huge shadow over the rest of both of their lives. It has even taken on a somewhat mythical status within the psychedelic community, as an incident which demonstrates both the intellectual brilliance and bravery of their truly megalomanic ambitions, and to some others the mental derangement that is possible through the reckless ingestion of too many powerful hallucinogens. Many years later Terence would reflect on the titanic magnitude of their wild ambitions:

"I was intrigued by his precision in invoking these ideas. ... I believed in the infinite, self-transforming power of the human mind and species, and I could suppose that there were parallel worlds and alternate dimensions. I could imagine any number of science-fiction possibilities, provided that I was not asked to believe that I was about to be present personally at their discovery or unleashing. But this is what Dennis was saying: We had somehow stumbled upon or been led to the trigger experience for the entire human world that would transform the ontological basis of reality so that the mind and matter everywhere would become the same thing and reflect the human will perfectly.

How could anyone conceive of such a thing? We had come to La Chorrera with a belief that if life and mind are possible, then the mysteries of the universe might well be inexhaustible. Yet something very passive, yet ever present, was there elaborating these ideas in our minds - something that we thought of for some days as "The Mushroom."

- Terence McKenna, *True Hallucinations*

Terence and Dennis were born and raised in Paonia, Colorado and were both brought up by their Irish descended father Joe, and Welsh descended mother Hadie. Dennis always believed that Terence's verbal lyricism and flamboyance was inherited from the Irish side of his ancestry. This was the genetic source of his legendary lilting "blarney." This was his yarn spinning capability which flavoured his always intellectually entertaining tales later in life. He was always a curious and maverick type thinker, who liked to investigate the world from his own unique perspective. Terence took a keen interest in various forms of natural history from an early age (including geology, botany, as well as a number of species of wildlife), and started many of his numerous collections in late childhood. At one point in his life, while he was lying low and on the run from interpol - he was being hunted for cannabis smuggling at the time - he even supported himself during these global travels through these specialist fields (such as collecting and selling rare butterflies in Indonesia). The best portrait of his young enthusiasms, and also his various scrapes with the authorities, is chronicled by his younger brother Dennis's recent autobiographical book: ***Brotherhood of the Screaming Abyss*** (their playful and witty take on their sometimes reckless psychedelic adventuring), a title that sometimes verged on being an accurate description of their dangerous entheogenic experimentation.

Terence and Dennis were close from an early age (even if Terence could be a typically mischievous older brother, and use him as a target for his dark humour). They were both blessed though with keen intelligences, and would also share a fascination with both science, and science-fiction. Terence was to also develop an early interest in altered states of consciousness: through a comparatively young reading of Aldous Huxley's two ground-breaking reflections on the effects of mescaline, the Native-American shamanic medicine. Those two books were titled: **The Doors of Perception** and **Heaven and Hell**. These books are still rated as crucial and pioneering works by the entheogenic community, and have lost none of their charm or eloquence with the passage of time. Huxley is still a figure of great interest, not just because or his praise of psychedelics, but also because of his vast knowledge and elucidation of non-denomination forms of mysticism, or the "perennial philosophy" as he also termed it. The fact that a figure of his intellectual esteem drew attention to these altered states of consciousness, and their resemblance to natural epiphanies that have been experienced and described by mystics throughout the ages, gave the subject an added authority. Before this, such shamanic practices (particularly in South America), had been dismissed by Western culture as simply primitive states of intoxication and delirium, and unworthy of scientific study. One of Huxley's most pivotal insights was that the brain might not simply be the reflector of external reality, but instead functioned as a "reducing valve" that in fact limited the perception of reality to a fraction of its true beauty and complexity. He pondered whether this had evolved as a defence mechanism for the biological survival of the organism. What the brain needed was to concentrate on its immediate surroundings in order to exist within a hostile environment. What psychedelics possibly allowed was a fleeting glimpse beneath this veil, to a true vision of the phenomenal world. He was also a very progressive intellectual figure, and a writer who was spiritual rather than religious, and still of great value today.

Terence was to also read a couple of influential *The Village Voice* magazine pieces, on the new research being undertaken on psilocybin magic mushrooms (then a completely new scientific field), and their effects on human consciousness. These early interests would go on to last a lifetime. When he was to move on to higher education, he began to first study art history at the *University of California, Berkeley*, but his interests were soon spreading to other more idiosyncratic topics such as "Tibetan painting and hallucinogenic shamanism." By this time he was already starting to build a vast library of books on a diversity of esoteric subjects, as well as a colourful library of personal psychedelic experiences too. There were few mind-altering substances that Terence was not personally acquainted with, and had appraised for their spiritual and scientific worth. He saw himself very much as a researcher, and a seeker of insights - solutions to the puzzles and mysteries of the mind and the universe. When Terence and Dennis were to reunite, when Dennis had came of age and was himself becoming independent, their paths would again converge and become forever entwined with these common interests. Even when their paths diverged again later in life, in order to follow their own individual career paths, this close bond was to still remain lifelong. As each was both a support and valuable influence on the other - and fellow psychonauts, looking for wisened guides in the magical, and sometimes perilous, realm of psychedelic exploration:

"We are not primarily biological, with mind emerging as a kind of iridescence, a kind of epiphenomenon at the higher levels of organization of biology. We are hyperspatial objects of some sort that cast a *shadow* onto matter. The shadow in matter is our physical organism. ... Both the psychedelic dream state and the waking psychedelic state acquire great import because they reveal to life a task: to become familiar with this dimension that is causing being, in order to be familiar with it at the moment of passing from life."

- Terence McKenna, **The Archaic Revival**

The two different callings they each eventually settled on had more to do with their different personalities and natures rather than any real differing ideological perspective - as the subjects that were to fascinate them still remained at the core of their character throughout their lives. Dennis was to eventually go back into higher education, and retrained to become a qualified and titled scientist. He gained a scientific Doctorate in Botanical Studies - and was to go on to become a well respected *ethnopharmacologist*. Terence was always a more maverick figure, and preferred to remain on the fringe of the scientific world. An established academic career was never really in Terence's temperament, he instead preferred to maintain his independence, and earn a living in a far more bohemian, but also unstable way. In the late Eighties and early Nineties he was to become increasingly more productive in terms of his literary output, with books like **True Hallucinations**, **Food of the Gods**, and **The Archaic Revival** becoming global selling titles. Because of these works he was also becoming a sought after personality within the public lecture world; where he could elaborate on his book's themes, and entrance audiences with his spellbinding monologues upon his favourite subjects. This was also a field that Terence particularly excelled at, because he was a brilliant orator, who possessed a wit and skill with the spoken language which is not always conveyed in his written work. This is not a criticism of his books, which were always profound and thought provoking; but not all great writers are also skilled with the spoken word as well. We are fortunate that his lifetime coincided with the age of the internet and other recording media - because later generations are now able to access many of his talks and speeches through this and other mediums. His popularity now is if anything growing, largely because of the appreciation of his verbal riffs on a number of colourful topics (YouTube is a clear indication of this trend). This verbal legacy may one day even overshadow his literary work:

"Because the fact is, what blinds us to the presence of alien intelligence is linguistic and cultural bias operating on ourselves. The world which we *perceive* is a tiny fraction of the world we *can* perceive, which is a tiny fraction of the *perceivable* world, you see. We operate on a very narrow slice based on cultural conventions. So the important thing, if synergizing progress is the notion to be maximised (and I think it's the notion to be maximised), is to try and locate the blind spot in the culture - the place where the culture isn't looking, because it dare not - because if it were to look there, its previous values would *dissolve*, you see. For Western Civilisation that place is the psychedelic experience as it emerges out of nature."

- Terence Mckenna, ***Understanding and Imagination in the Light of Nature***

Terence is sometimes viewed as a psychedelic successor to Timothy Leary, but in many ways this is a somewhat distorted picture of Terence's goals and legacy. For Terence was far less reckless, or even public about what he considered was the true role of psychedelics in society, and often called for the "intelligent" employment of their use. He considered them both as tools of enlightenment, when properly prepared for and consumed (but also potentially very hazardous when approached complacently, or simply naively), and he also recognised that probably "they weren't for everybody."

This testimony is no doubt informed by his own, and his brother's experiences at "La Chorrera" early on in their adventurous lives, and which was surely the single most important event that catalysed their two different directions. It also seemed to overshadow both of their attempts to make sense of this bizarre period as well. This event took place in the early Seventies. In 1971, after the death of their mother, they decided to make a rather spirited but reckless expedition, with three friends and fellow travellers, into the depths of the Colombian Amazon, in search of the reputed brew of the indigenous shamanic culture called *oo-koo-he*, a liquid form of DMT, and close relative of *ayahuasca*. This was known to be a mixed plant brew that had been used for hundreds, if not thousands of years as a vehicle for the attainment of sacred knowledge. Because of their unsuccessful and probably dangerous investigations into locating this mysterious brew when they finally arrived at this elusive geographical destination, they became to a certain extent distracted by the abundance of another form of psychotropic fungi instead. This was the huge *Stropharia cubensis,* which was common in this particular area of the forest, and instead became the new and unexpected focus of their psychedelic mission. This was to not only divert them from their original scheme, but also throw them into a situation that was to completely consume the rest of their time in this somewhat obscure and mysterious region. Terence and Dennis began to consume this powerful hallucinogen on a regular dietary basis (to the concern and consternation of their friends, who had become increasingly detached from them). As their theories of their purposes and goals became more and more extravagant and megalomanic, this would increasingly divide the camp and fuel suspicions of psychosis and delusions of grandeur. During this time Terence and Dennis felt that they were in contact with some form of alien intelligence, which was both encouraging, and schooling them with forms of hidden cosmic knowledge. They were unsure as to what the exact source of this disincarnate intelligence was, whether was the *Spirit of the Mushroom*, an *alien entity* which was communicating with them through this shamanic medium, or even the divine and universal *Logos* itself, the ethereal embodiment of religious experience. These discussions were to eventually spiral into disagreements that led to the parting of the two brothers from the rest of the group:

"As the evening wore on, our conversation drifted toward and around the possibility of violating normal physics, discussing it in terms of a psychological verse a naive/realist view of shamanic phenomena. We were especially interested in the obsidian liquids that *ayahuasqueros* are said to produce on the surface of their skins and use to look into time. The idea of a kind of hologramatic alchemical fluid, a self-generated liquid crystal ball, seemed to me very strange and somehow compelling. The question of whether or not such things are possible is actually a more gut issue in disguise: Is what we moderns have remaining to learn about the nature of reality slight and will it require only light fine-tuning of our current way of looking at things; or do we understand very little, missing the point entirely about the nature of our situation in being? I found myself arguing that reality is made of language and that we somehow had to step outside the cultural prison of language to confront a reality behind appearances. "If you would strike, strike through the mask!" That sort of thing."

- Terence McKenna, **True Hallucinations**

At this point Dennis's behaviour was becoming extremely eccentric and erratic. Terence was to describe some of the truly bizarre and astonishing things he witnessed during this period of time, such as the conjuring of a tiny planet for them to observe, staggering pieces of information Dennis was able to recall, and eventually to witness a UFO, high up above him in the Amazon forest. During this time Terence was even unsure if the staggering ambitions Dennis was proclaiming were in fact becoming true, or were simply evidence of psychosis and mental breakdown. There was for some days a confusion as to whether they had succeeded, and altered the whole fabric of reality. When it became increasingly obvious that the universe had not been transformed, it was instead clear that it was Dennis who had become divorced from reality, and his bizarre behaviour was more symptomatic of a complete mental dissolution, and the group feared that the damage done might even become irreparable. It was clear that Dennis was in a state of utter confusion and totally alienation from reality. Terence, however, fought the rest of the group's urge to contact the authorities and ask for urgent medical help and treatment - fearing the longer they left him in this condition, the more likely he would be to lose any sanity left in him. Terence was able to resist this move, he was able to take full responsibility for him, and thought that Dennis was undergoing some sort of shamanic dissolution, and that he would need to work through this psychological process himself, with his support. He felt that direct medical intervention with other chemical bombardments to his psyche could be utterly disastrous to his fragile mind. Thankfully, after a number of days Dennis would finally begin to recover, and in hindsight he believes his brother made the right call. But this was a very frightening episode though, and an event that is still tinged with a strange confusion. Terence was always slightly perturbed by what happened in those few baffling days. Was it simply the disturbed ravings of two intoxicated psychonauts, who had strayed too far over the edge, and lost all their groundings in reality. Or simply a failed experiment, a noble quest that still beckons mankind with the tantalising promise of immortality, and a total uprooting of our understanding of the universe:

"In this notion we were following Jung, who early on realised the flying saucer is an image of the self, the suppressed psychic totality that lurks behind the apparent dualism of mind and nature. We thought that the field of mind and its will toward the good could be templated onto the genetic engines of life. The hope was that out of biology, Tantra could summon the reality of the living stone, the chimerical unicorn of the alchemical quest made at last to lay his head in the maiden's lap. We dreamed in short, of a union of Spirit and Matter.

The dead: We believed that hyper-carbolation was to be the shamanic defeat of death, that those doorways through which the dead enter daily were to be finally thrown open to a hyper-carbolated humanity, which would then have freedom of movement to and from an eternity in which all the members of the species existed as a living reality. The presence of giants from the human past - Carl Jung, Newton, and Nabokov, Bruno, Pythagoras, and Heraclitus - was an overwhelming and all-inclusive intuition that we shared and could not ignore."

- Terence McKenna, ***True Hallucinations***

Dennis was fortunate to make a full recovery (even if it was to take weeks instead of days according to his autobiography), but this obviously traumatic episode did not in fact scare him off the study of psychedelics, but instead led to a lifetime engagement with this controversial field. He afterwards believed that what he needed was a much more scientific grounding in the subject, and a clear objective appraisal of the complex chemistry that was in operation. He is today considered one of the global authorities in this area, and his reputation is bolstered by his considerable qualifications and academic achievements. After this juncture of his life, however, his close contact and rapport with his brother was to lessen, as their life's seemed to be pulling them both in slightly different directions. While Dennis began to pursue a far more orthodox career path within the scientific and academic world, Terence was to drift off into a more unstable, but eventually more public role, which was to see him become the more socially famous, or possibly more infamous of the two brothers.

One of the books that was coauthored by the two brothers at this critical and intense period of their lives was **The Invisible Landscape**. This was the book that was to first espouse one of Terence McKenna's most controversial ideas, but also the one that he believed was his most significant contribution to the understanding of time and the universe. That was his theory of *Timewave Zero*. Though the book was a joint venture, Dennis would later distance himself from it slightly, and imply that it was "mainly Terence's idea," and probably shouldn't be taken too seriously. *Timewave Zero* was their prediction that the universe was in fact heading towards an *Omega Point*, or a singularity event, which would be the concrescence of all mind and matter as it was being inextricably pulled towards this final destination point. They believed that the *I Ching* (also known as the King Wen sequence), the ancient Chinese model of time, had contained within it the hidden key through which humanity could see these patterns or periods of anomalous time encoded. They used this formula to mathematically translate its movement as an encoded number sequence, and plotted this irregular numerical trajectory as a graph. This strange model was then analysed to see if it corresponded with any type of significant pattern in human history. Their mathematical model was said to correspond to seismic waves of "novel" historical change, and so christened *Novelty Theory* by the two brothers. They believed that the patterns on the graph in fact lined pretty clearly with key major events which defined human history, when something new arrived in the world and changed the direction of its course. Critics would understandably question how you can ever scientifically measure "novelty" though, which appears a purely subjective concept; certainly when applied to history. This theory was elaborated with great mathematical precision and even developed into a computer programme, and Terence was obviously infatuated by the theory. The central idea was that even if the universe was not created by a singularity (which is the central tenant of all the Big Bang theories within cosmology, and one certainly not discounted by Terence), then it was certainly headed for one - this was the great attractor, pulling all time lines towards it with its irresistible teleological gravitational force:

"Our theory is one of a progressive spiral involution of time toward a concrescence, rather than a theory of a static hierarchy of waves, eternally expressed on many levels. This is because the terminal positions in the King Wen wave naturally quantify as zero states. ... This results in a progressive drop of valuations toward the zero state as any epoch enters its terminal phase. Only in the situation of final concrescence does the valuation on all levels become zero. In fact, the quantified definition of absolute concrescence is that it is the zero point in the quantified wave-hierarchy.

- Terence McKenna and Dennis McKenna, *The Invisible Landscape*

Their conception of the universe was that time, mind and matter were all being inextricably drawn into a terminal point which they viewed as *The Eschaton* (Terence was particularly influenced by *Whitehead* in this respect). This was to be the ultimate convergence of Time, Spirit and Matter as it is being inextricably pulled towards this impending climax - the transformative destiny of all life within the universe. His theory was that time itself would seem to accelerate - as cascading new forms of technological change and intellectual progress (as well physical laws) were to simultaneously gain momentum and coalesce as this singularity approached:

"Everything is flowing together. The "autopoietic lapis," the alchemical stone at the end of time, coalesces when everything flows together. When the laws of physics are obviated, the universe disappears, and what is left is the tightly bound plenum, the monad, able to express itself for itself, rather than only able to cast a shadow into *physis* as its reflection."

- Terence McKenna, ***New Maps of Hyperspace***

Looking at human history, this gradation of social change does seem to be an interesting metaphor for this process in action. The speed of technological development certainly demonstrates this principle, with such barometers as economic and political change, as well as discoveries in the fields of science also accelerating exponentially. The technological changes presently underway in modern society not only seem to be accelerating at a pace that previous generations would have found unthinkable, but also seem to have a momentum which is itself beyond our control. Terence was to view these developments with a mixture of both awe and anticipation. His belief was that this process was not only well underway, but quickly heading towards towards a transcendental climax:

"The universe is being pulled from the future toward a goal that is as inevitable as a marble reaching the bottom of a bowl when you release it up near the rim. If you do that, you know the marble will roll down the bowl - down, down, down - until it eventually comes to rest at the lowest energy state, which is at the bottom of the bowl. That's precisely my model of human history."

- Terence McKenna, ***Understanding and Imagination in the Light of Nature***

What was quite alarming was that after they had finished all their calculations and attempts to best correlate their model to historical epochs, the end date they were to settle on was strikingly in accord with another model of the mechanics of time: the ancient Mayan Calendar. They claim that they were to arrive at this date completely independently, and were only made aware of this coincidence afterwards (though the story goes that they secretly tweaked their model to slyly add a little credibility to their hypothesis). Scholars would later point to the fact that the end of the Mayan Long Count calendar did not necessarily spell any form of cosmic cataclysm, or indeed the end of time, but rather the end of a huge cycle of time. This was a *circular* process of change that marked the end of this *rotation* of deep time, rather than a destination or singularity. At the time though, the brothers were sure that it heralded an event of titanic significance, and thought that such a coincidence was itself surely beyond fortuitous:

"The end date is the point of maximised novelty in the wave and is the only point in the entire wave that has a quantified value of zero. We arrived at this particular end date without knowledge of the Mayan Calendar, and it was only after we noticed that the historical data seemed to fit best with the wave if this end date was chosen that we were informed that the end date that we had deduced was in fact the end of the Mayan Calendar."

- Terence McKenna and Dennis McKenna, **The Invisible Landscape**

Terence claimed a number of times that this was really one of his only creative intellectual contributions to the world, and that this prediction would either mean he was an important social prophet or possibly "barking mad." When 21.12.2012, came and went with so little fuss, his critics would amusedly opt for the latter conclusion. But this was in many ways to lose the point of Terence McKenna. In **Brotherhood of the Screaming Abyss**, Dennis (already distancing himself from these much younger apocalyptic prophecies), was to reflect that Terence's real contribution to the world was not only as a daring and imaginative thinker (who could obviously also be extremely wrong), but also as a witty and incisive social critic. These are the gifts which will probably be his real legacy, and many of his greatest admirers were always a little skeptical about *Timewave Zero*. But to them this was irrelevant to his other talents and achievements, which included a very incisive outsider's eye on what was going on in politics and culture within modern societies. Insights that were usually tinged with his trademark wit and humour (a sense of humour that could also be deployed on himself and his sometimes extravagant claims). These insights are scattered throughout not only his literary works, but also his lectures, and will no doubt remain valuable to anyone willing to think for themselves, and willing to truly look at aspects of our irrational behaviour:

"Most unsettling of all is this: the content of television is not a vision but a manufactured data stream that can be sanitised to "protect" or impose cultural values. Thus we are confronted with an addictive and all-pervasive drug that delivers an experience whose message is whatever those who deal the drug wish it to be. ... Yet no drug in history has so quickly or completely isolated the entire culture of its users from contact with reality. And no drug in history has so completely succeeded in remaking in its own image the values of the culture that it has infected."

- Terence McKenna, ***Food of the Gods***

One of Terence's most interesting theories is known as the "stoned ape theory" of evolution, and posited the possibly crucial influence *Psilocybe cubensis* may have played in our evolution (an idea Bill Hicks was to also to find so appealing). His contention, elaborated chiefly in one of his most popular titles: ***Food of the Gods***, was that when our ancestors were forced into new dietary experimentation, due to massive environmental change; they would have discovered this new food source. He believed that the biological effects of this psychotropic fungi had properties that may have given its consumer an evolutionary advantage over other members of the species, and could have helped facilitate the gradual transformation from *Homo erectus* to *Homo sapiens*. Terence believed that low doses of this hallucinogen have been known to improve visual acuity, which would have been a significant advantage to a species which were at the time *hunter-gathers*. At medium doses, mushrooms are also considered to be a sexual stimulant, which would have also have been a spur to sire more offspring - thereby increasing the user's genetic legacy. At higher doses, it also known to have an ego dissolving function on the psyche: this could have played a critical function in group bonding within the wider species or tribe, cementing relations and bringing about group cohesion within a hostile environment. Finally, and possibly most importantly, at high doses, psychedelics are known to produce transcendental and boundary dissolving states, which could have triggered the species first religious experiences (in fact some researchers believe that such states could be the bedrock of conceptual as well as ethical thinking too). Terence had always been fascinated by the origin and role of language within human culture, and was always intrigued by the link between conceptual thought, and the birth of the vocalisation of thought processes in this context. Were our first attempts at elemental communication an effort to communicate the ineffable experiences that were first encountered in such transcendental altered states? Terence often expressed the idea that there was a link within various religious parables (such as the *Fruit of Knowledge of Good and Evil* in the Garden of Eden), and mankind's own experiences with consumed entheogens. Could this have been the real source of such metaphors about the higher realms of sacred knowledge through the ingestion of certain plants? Were the seeds of the human imagination and culture sown by this specific interaction? Terence thought it certainly possible:

"Our capacity for cognitive and linguistic activity is related to the size and organization of the human brain. Neural structures concerned with conceptualization, visualization, signification, and association are highly developed in our species. Through the act of speaking vividly, we enter into a flirtation with the domain of the imagination. The ability to associate sounds, or the small mouth noises of language, with meaningful internal images is a synesthesic activity. The most recently evolved areas of the human brain, Broca's area and the neocortex, are devoted to the control of symbol and language processing. ... Cognitive activity within a group usually means the elaboration and manipulation of symbols and language. Although this occurs in many species, within the human species it is especially well developed. Our immense power to manipulate symbols and language gives us our unique position in the natural world. The power of our magic and our science arises out of our commitment to group mental activity, symbol sharing, meme replication (the spreading of ideas), and the telling of tall tales."

- Terence McKenna, ***Food of the Gods***

Terence found these ideas not only beguiling, he also believed this highlighted a symbiotic balance that man had once shared with nature. A relationship that was now seriously undermined, and this imbalance was fuelling man's seriously destructive attitude towards its environment. Perhaps mankind may have lost a crucial sense of this sensitive balance, through the demonisation of certain plants and fungi which had once helped facilitate its psychological development and wider intuition - as well as a far deeper understanding of its place within the *whole* of Nature. He considered the loss of some of these boundary and ego dissolving states as symptomatic of the species more pathological behaviour, not only towards its own fragile ecosystems, but also towards its own species (mankind's track record of inter-species slaughter and genocide is a pretty graphic example). He looked at the products which are now culturally condoned and socially approved (such as sugar, alcohol, and tobacco), and considered them not only to be far more biologically dangerous and self-destructive than most illegal psychedelics, but in many ways indicative of their societies own toxic and schizophrenic values.

From the early Eighties on, Terence began to discuss and explore these topical questions within the public lecture circuit, on campuses and at conferences. Here he was to acquire the reputation of an exciting and original thinker, with a rare talent for mesmerising an audience with his florid monologues. His depth of knowledge of nature was almost as extensive as his wide experience with all forms of psychedelics - and he had an uncanny knack of being able to elucidate verbally the essence of these experiences, and convey vocally their often ineffable visual nature. He was recognised as a very challenging and insightful communicator, and would also draw around him other scientists and intellectuals who were attracted to his ever questioning and curious style. Two of the most interesting of these collaborators was biologist Rupert Sheldrake, and mathematician Ralph Abraham. These three good friends would help create "Trialogues" within an open discussion forum - in order to dynamise their public debates on key issues. These debates ranged from topics such as scientific epistemology, the nature of language, and even the phenomenon of alien contact and communication. Some of these debates were later published under the title: **Trialogues at the Edge of the West** in book form. These dialogues were often fueled by the desire to investigate both the limits and triumphs of the scientific method, and also to find creative new ways to interpret the anomalous phenomena which the human mind has experienced through altered states of consciousness. Such as, what is the reality of the reported incidences of entity contact which have been described throughout human history; contact with non-human and often otherworldly intelligences? Are they simply projections of the Jungian collective unconsciousness from man's inner psyche, are they contact with some other form of Gaian Overmind, or even more incredibly - communication with some form of extraterrestrial intelligence or interdimensional beings? This was a subject that was always beguiling, and particularly close to Terence's heart:

"This discussion will revolve around the exotic theme of discarnate intelligences and nonhuman entities. These entities seem to occupy a kind of undefined ontological limbo. Whatever their status in the world, their persistence in human experience and folklore is striking. The phenomenon of their existence is not something unusual or statistically rare. In all times and all places, with the possible exception of Western Europe for the past two hundred years, a social commerce between human beings and various types of discarnate entities, or nonhuman intelligences, was taken for granted."

- Ralph Abraham, Terence McKenna, Rupert Sheldrake, ***Trialogues at the Edge of the West***

Terence was of course familiar with just about the whole range of the psychedelic spectrum, and was also was known to be quite fearless in tasting the extreme limits of what these states had to offer the human mind. He had also coauthored a book with his brother on the cultivation of psilocybin magic mushrooms, and a guide to their psychedelic usage. He was also no stranger to LSD either (though not a huge fan), as well as many of the more novel and rare entheogenic plant hallucinogens. There was, however, one substance that to him represented the *apotheosis* of the psychedelic experience. An extremely rare drug compared to other "street" compounds, and whose existence seemed in many ways a kind of mythical holy grail to the curious psychonaut. This molecule was only fairly recently understood to be the visionary component of *ayahuasca*, the ancient shamanic brew that had existed for hundreds if not thousands of years in the Amazon basin. This and its derivatives are what the McKenna brothers had gone in search of in their now infamous "La Chorrera" trip. *Ayahuasca* is the liquid form of this compound and is metabolised much slower by the body, and also lasts much longer through this method of ingestion. In its purer form, it can be administered intravenously, or far more commonly, smoked. It was through this method that Terence was to first casually encounter "the Spirit Molecule," and was left absolutely dumbfounded. Although the experience, even at maximum dosage, only lasts fifteen minutes (it is sometimes known as the "businessman's trip" because the whole experience is over within the length of a work day lunch break), the speed of its action and the utter power of its effects were to shock even him. That compound was N,N-DMT, or as it is also known *Dimethyltryptamine*. The first time he smoked it, he in fact thought that he must have overdosed and died, because you "couldn't go this far into the Bardo and return." He found himself within a matter of seconds transported to an utterly alien and autonomous dimension, and what's more, this dimension was inhabited:

"Once smoked, the onset of the experience begins in about fifteen seconds. One falls immediately into a trance. One's eyes are closed and one hears a sound like ripping cellophane, like someone crumpling up plastic film and throwing it away. A friend of mine suggests this is our radio entelechy ripping out of the organic matrix. An ascending tone is heard. Also present is the normal hallucinogenic modality, a shifting geometric surface of migrating and changing coloured forms. At the synaptic site of the activity, all available bond sites are being occupied, and one experiences the mode shift occurring over a period of about thirty seconds. At that point one arrives in a place that defies description ... The room is actually going around, and in that space one feels like a child, though one has come out somewhere in eternity."

- Terence McKenna, ***The Archaic Revival***

Terence had always been fascinated with the idea that psilocybin magic mushrooms might facilitate a method of communication with other life forms across the universe. People who ingest large quantities (the famous McKenna "heroic" doses) often report experiences with some form of extraterrestrial intelligence, as well as hyper futuristic visions of alien technology (such as flying saucers in the case of Bill Hicks). Terence had also flirted with the idea that mushroom spores themselves might be of extraterrestrial origin, and have been transported through the cosmos and seeded on the earth, and that the information accessed was genetically encoded within its DNA. This idea is not as wild as it seems, for many highly acclaimed scientists such as Francis Crick, the

Nobel prize winner and co-discoverer of DNA, believed that DNA was far too complicated to have spontaneously evolved on the Earth (within its time frame). He believed (along with a number of respected scientists) in the theory of *Panspermia,* in which life itself was seeded from sources outside of our planet. This DMT form of alien contact though was significantly different. What shocked Terence most about the DMT phenomenology, was that it seemed to have no psychological effects on a person's *psyche* at all, you mentally "arrived there with all your groceries," but you were just simply transported to *another dimension.* A dimension buzzing with utterly bizarre local inhabitants. When asked if DMT was dangerous, he replied that physically it was one of the safest drugs on the planet, within half-an-hour of taking it you "felt fine" and were "taking phone calls" as if nothing had happened. The only real danger was that you might "die of *astonishment.*" Whatever these beings were, they were not only alien to our physical planet, but also foreign to our universe:

"These entities are dynamically contorting topological modules that are somehow distinct from the surrounding background, which is itself undergoing a continuous transformation. ... The tryptamine Munchkins come, these hyper-dimensional machine-elf entities, and they bathe one in love. It's not erotic but is open-hearted. It certainly feels good. These beings are like fractal reflections of some previously and suddenly autonomous part of one's own psyche. ... This happened to me twenty seconds after I smoked DMT on a particular day in 1966. I was appalled. Until then I had thought that I had my ontological categories intact. I had taken LSD before, yet this came upon me like a bolt from the blue. I came down and said (and I said it many times). "I cannot believe this; this is impossible, this is completely impossible." There was a declension of gnosis that proved to me in a moment that right here and now, one quanta away, there is a raging universe of active intelligence that is transhuman, hyper-dimensional, and extremely alien."

- Terence McKenna, **The Archaic Revival**

In this way Terence would later go on to become DMT's most vocal and iconic Western exponent (William Burrough's could technically claim to be its first Western pioneer, but his experiences were to become terrifying and he rejected its use). Because he came to champion this rare psychedelic publicly above all others, his name will now probably be forever associated with it. Though he could spellbind his audiences with these incredible tales, the compound began to acquire a kind of mythical status to many in the psychedelic community. This was largely to do with the almost impossible task of obtaining it, as it was such a rare and sometimes feared commodity, even within those circles that actively pursued these underground substances. Instead most of audience had simply to make do with Terence's own spectacular accounts. The fantastic folklore of DMT had begun.

Sadly, as Terence's message and ideas were gaining increased interest and diffusion, he had began to suffer more and more severe migraines, until one night he was struck with full blown seizures, and very nearly died. He was then devastatingly diagnosed with a particularly aggressive form of brain tumour. Though he stoically endured months of medical treatment (such as gamma radiation) to battle its relentless onslaught on his wild and witty mind, it was alas, a fight he could not win. He passed away on April 3rd 2000, surrounded by his family and loved ones, including his brother Dennis. In the final personal interview he was to give to *Erik Davis*, he described with quiet pathos his reflections on his own mortality:

"I always thought death would come on the freeway in a few horrifying moments, so you'd have no time to sort it out. Having months and months to look at it and think about it and to talk to people and hear what they have to say, it's a kind of blessing. It's certainly an opportunity to grow up and get a grip and sort it all out. Just being told by an unsmiling guy in a white coat that you're going to be dead in four months definitely turns on the lights ... It makes life rich and poignant.

When it first happened, and I got these diagnoses, I could see the light of eternity, a la William Blake, shining through every leaf. I mean, a bug walking across the ground moved me to tears."

But as Terence's light sadly waned and faded, the story of DMT, did not also end. Because just as his ideas and hypotheses were attracting more public interest and curiosity, history was to take an unexpected turn. And science too was about to independently take a more serious investigation into this mysterious compound: *"The Spirit Molecule."*

IV

"This bare and simple infinity, or the absolute notion, may be called the ultimate nature of life, the soul of the world, the universal life-blood, which courses everywhere, and whose flow is neither disturbed nor checked by any obstructing distinction, but is itself every distinction that arises, as well as that into which all distinctions are dissolved; pulsating within itself, but ever motionless, shaken to its depths, but still at rest. It is self-identical, for the distinctions are tautological; they are distinctions that are none. This self-identical reality stands, therefore, in relation purely to itself."

- G.W.F. Hegel, *The Phenomenology of Mind*

Chapter 4

Realms of the Fantastic

The Phenomenology of DMT

"Oh, DMT, yeah, it's called dimethyltryptamine, it's produced by your pineal gland. It's actually a gland that lives in the center of your brain. It's the craziest drug ever. It's the most potent psychedelic known to man. ... But the craziest thing about it is it's natural, and your brain produces it every night as you sleep. You know when you sleep, during the time you're in heavy REM sleep, and right before human *death*, your brain pumps out heavy doses of dimethyltryptamine. Nobody knows what dreaming is all about, nobody knows why dreaming is important, but dreaming is hugely important. If you don't dream you'll go fuckin' crazy and you'll die. While you're dreaming, while you're in heavy REM sleep, you are going through a psychedelic trip. And very few people know about this. It's been documented. There's a great book on it called **DMT: The Spirit Molecule**, by a doctor, a doctor named *Rick Strassman*. And he did all these clinical studies at the *University of New Mexico* on it, and you take this shit and literally you are transported into another *fuckin' dimension*. I don't mean you feel like you're in another dimension, I mean like you're *in* another dimension ... there's fucking *complex geometric patterns moving in synchronistic order* through the air all around you in three dimensional space. And it's like they're arteries, except there's not blood pumping through them, there's fuckin' light, pulsating lights with no boundaries and you couldn't really understand it ... and there's an *alien* communicating with me. There's a dude who looks like, sort of like a Thai Buddha, except he's made entirely of energy, and there's no, there's like no outline to him. He's just one thing, and he's concentrating on me, and he's trying to tell me: "Not to give in to astonishment! Just relax, and try to experience this." And I'm like: "You gotta be fucking shittin' me!" ... And I'm a stand-up comedian, you know, and as a stand-up comedian we pride ourselves on being able to describe things, so I'm like: "How the fuck am I going to talk about this?" It's insane ... And there's all these fucking complex patterns moving around, and this guy's looking at me in the eye, and I'm fuckin' freaking out, and it lasts for about five minutes. And when it's over, when it's over after five minutes, you're like: "What the fuck is that?"

This is a slice of the dialogue from a conversation recorded on a radio talk show, the subject, and the response, were completely spontaneous - but has now become the most famous soliloquy on DMT ever given. It has already drawn over three-and-a-half million hits on YouTube, and shows no sign of abating there. This outburst was simply, and unexpectedly, prompted by a question asked on a call-in radio show featuring the touring American stand-up comedian *Joe Rogan,* and sparked this lengthy monologue about his own personal experience. The question was in fact aimed at an incident involving Joe and another superb stand-up comic and friend - *Doug Stanhope.* That was the time that Joe introduced Doug to the close and even more powerful cousin of dimethyltryptamine - 5 MeO DMT. But Joe used the opportunity to expound on the subject of N,N-DMT, and give his thoughts on what he considered to be not only one of the most incredible experiences of his life, but also one of the most perplexing and intriguing subjects facing humanity.

Joe Rogan and Doug Stanhope were not only old friends, they both also belong to that fine lineage of great American stand-ups, a genealogy that stretched back through Bill Hicks, Sam Kinison and

Richard Pryor. Guys that were not only gut bustingly funny, but also had something important to say. These descendents could also include such performers as Chris Rock, Louis CK, and George Carlin. Both Joe Rogan and Doug Stanhope were huge admirers of Bill Hicks as a comedian, but they also shared other common interests too; notably psychedelics. Some might feel that Doug Stanhope is possibly the funniest (and to some others also the most depraved) comedian on the planet, but Joe Rogan is possibly the more intriguing, in terms of the scope of his interests. As he is not only a stand-up comedian, but also an extremely accomplished Mixed Martial Artist (and equally famous UFC commentator), as well as being a TV presenter and unlikely psychedelic spokesman. His introduction to DMT was through a highly experienced and scholarly psychedelic researcher (and nucleus of GnosticMedia) *Jan Irvin*. This event was to have a profound effect on Joe, and has triggered an interest in many forms of altered states of consciousness, an interest that could probably be called a passion. He has also become an aficionado of marijuana, isolation tanks, as well as tryptamine hallucinogens, in particular - DMT. His lengthy riff on this once obscure topic was to also spark interest in the book: **DMT: The Spirit Molecule** which chronicled the US government's first legally sanctioned research into psychedelics in nearly twenty years. And what's more, research that was conducted using one of the most powerful hallucinogens known to man - *dimethyltryptamine*.

Rick Strassman was born on February 8th, 1952, in Los Angeles, and trained as a doctor in Psychiatry, but ended up specialising in *psychopharmacology*. During his training years he was attracted to the practises of spirituality, in particular Buddhism, and became a practising disciple for many years. He was also interested in the *altered states of consciousness* which were being achieved by people experimenting with various psychedelic compounds (during the Fifties and early Sixties there was huge excitement about the potential therapeutic benefits of these newly discovered drugs, *like LSD*, and what they may teach us about brain chemistry). Rick was curious as to what the biological mechanisms might be for explaining these transcendent mystical states - reported throughout various religious practices, such as deep meditation, and wondered if there was a distinct chemical basis for such experiences. Towards the end of the Sixties though, through a combination of reckless academic misconduct, combined with social fears about their widespread abuse, these psychedelic compounds became outlawed, and any academic looking to explore this controversial field risked instant career suicide.

For many years Rick shelved these interests and instead pursued other lines of psychiatric medicine, and only later began academic research into such areas as the regulatory functions of melatonin on consciousness (though this was indeed related to these interests), a compound that regulates our sleep patterns. During this period he was to privately develop his own theories of what may be the biological mechanism for these altered forms of consciousness, and all his research pointed towards one organ that seemed to be the most likely candidate for the source of endogenous DMT - the mysterious *pineal gland*. It was known by this time that two of the most potent hallucinogens so far recognised by science - 5 MeO DMT and N,N-DMT, were in fact both produced naturally by the body. They were endogenous to not only the human organism, but also present in every mammal that has so far been tested. The most obvious question has to be: "What are these chemicals doing in our bodies? What function do they have within our consciousness? And where is it being produced?" To Rick, N,N-DMT's (at the time the exclusive subject of his research) most likely source of origin was the enigmatic pineal gland. This mysterious and tiny organ is located at the center of our brain, and is one of the only *singular* organs within it (the supposed unity of consciousness is one of reasons that *Rene Descartes* saw the pineal as the *seat of the soul*). The pineal is also believed to be the famous "third eye" of numerous occult and esoteric sects. The pineal has many biological features which also make it appear as a type of "inner eye" and in some rare species the pineal even has a cornea, a retina, and a lens, making it *literally* a third eye. What the exact function of the pineal is in brain chemistry is still *definitively* unresolved, but to Rick it was the best candidate for the chemistry of *altered states of consciousness*:

"The pineal gland contains the necessary building blocks to make DMT. For example, it possesses the highest levels of serotonin anywhere in the body, and serotonin is a crucial precursor for pineal melatonin. The pineal also has the ability to convert serotonin to tryptamine, a critical step in DMT formation.

The unique enzymes that convert serotonin, melatonin, or tryptamine into psychedelic compounds also are present in extraordinary high concentrations in the pineal. These enzymes, the *methyltransferases*, attach a methyl group - that is, one carbon and three hydrogens - onto other molecules, thus *methylating* them. Simply methylate tryptamine twice, and we have di-methyl-tryptamine, or DMT. Because it possesses the high levels of the enzymes and precursors, the pineal is the most reasonable place for DMT formation to occur. Surprisingly, no one has ever looked for DMT in the pineal."

- Rick Strassman, **DMT: The Spirit Molecule**

As Rick's ideas about the pineal being the source of endogenous DMT developed, some of the anecdotal aspects of this strange organ also aroused his curiosity, such as the fact that the pineal is known to form on the forty-ninth day of fetus gestation, the time when the sex of the infant is also determined (and coincidentally the time that Buddhism believes the soul enters the body). For many years after the publication of his fascinating book, Rick has had to endure the criticism that his theory of the pineal as the natural source of DMT production was pure speculation, and was so far scientifically unproven. However, recently the *Cottonwood Research Foundation*, an institute that is dedicated to consciousness research (and an organisation Rick is heavily involved with), has finally proved the existence of DMT within the pineal gland of live rodents. As rodents have very similar functioning brains to our own, this essentially *verifies* the pineal DMT hypothesis. This is of *huge* significance to not only scientific research into brain chemistry;

but also to those researchers into the various religious denominations that have venerated the pineal throughout history (a subject that Anthony Peake has explored in great detail in one of the most interesting books on DMT so far written: ***The Infinite Mindfield***).

In the late Eighties, Rick finally decided that he would attempt to end this psychedelic research impasse, and applied officially to terminate this twenty year spell of scientific research prohibition. His proposal was to run clinical trials of DMT at the *University of New Mexico School of Medicine in Albuquerque*, where he was based. For this he had to endure months and months of paperwork and bureaucratic negotiations, in order to get approval from the various bodies that regulated this tightly controlled field. Much to his own surprise, and eventual relief, his effort paid off, and he was finally given the go ahead to run clinical trials (Rick framed the research to look at basically the biological reactions to the chemical, but in truth it was the *consciousness* reports he was after). Between 1990 and 1995 he administered approximately 400 doses (of varying strengths) to 60 volunteers. They were carefully screened for their past psychedelic experience and mental health, and were generally drawn from a cross section of well educated professionals with some experience of hallucinogens. Rick was privately hoping to gain a greater understanding of the chemical's relationship to religious, mystical, and possibly even near-death experiences (itself a fairly new and exciting field), and to hopefully also use his psychiatric training to help with any personal therapeutic issues that might surface. He was quietly hoping that the chemical might help the participants unlock and resolve any personal or emotional issues that might be buried deep within their own psyche:

"I expected to see many volunteers working through emotional and psychological conflicts during these studies. Sessions of this nature might help prepare the way for psychedelic-drug-assisted psychotherapy in patients. We would note how DMT affected volunteers in potentially beneficial ways, then build those effects into any subsequent psychological treatment protocol."

- Rick Strassman, **DMT: The Spirit Molecule**

At the beginning of the trials, these personal psychological features did surface, but as the experiment continued, a shocking new phenomenon also arose. During the lower doses, individual emotional content certainly did manifest itself, in accordance with Rick's expectations. Various psychological, and psychoanalytical models were employed to try to decipher and frame the meaning of these psychological states, in a bid to accurately interpret them, and help alert the volunteer to any underlying personal problems that they might be highlighting. However, when the dose strengths were increased, these experiences started to move towards completely new and entirely unexpected territory. The environment that the participants were being suddenly transported to took on a very different qualitative feel. To Rick's concern and confusion, these reports pointed towards *parallel alternate realities*:

"This terrain is not so easy to recognise or understand because the experiences are less clearly related to thoughts, feelings, and bodies of our volunteers. Rather, they suggest freestanding, independent levels of existence about which we are at most only dimly aware. These reports challenge our world view, and they raise the emotional intensity of the debate: "Is it a dream? A hallucination? Or is it real?" "Where are these places? Inside or out?" ... Certainly the spaces in which volunteers found themselves were highly unusual. However, more important was the meaning or the feeling, the information, associated with where they were. Of course, once other "life-forms" began to appear in those spaces, it was difficult not to be swept up in their existence ..."

- Rick Strassman, **DMT: The Spirit Molecule**

As the case studies (especially at the high-end doses) began to mount, Rick would find it increasingly difficult to explain them through the prism of psychiatric models of consciousness that he was schooled in. His attempts to decipher and decode them using these analytical methods were increasingly met with resistance and incomprehension from his patients, who were frustrated at his inability to take them at their own word. To them the reality of these encounters were both confounding, bizarre, but unmistakably *real*. Only when he finally accepted these accounts as authentic did his volunteers feel comfortable enough to open up to him, and give the fullest account of their experiences, and what their true meaning might be. This was to force Rick to fundamentally re-appraise his own interpretation of what he was learning from his study, and even rethink his own worldviews:

"Lack of open dialogue about these issues makes it much more difficult to even imagine enlarging our view of the reality of non-material realms using scientific methods. What would happen to the study of spirit realms if we could access them reliably using molecules like DMT?

In addition to questions regarding the existence of non-material or spiritual worlds, we also must consider expanding the notion of what we may perceive in them. Can our spiritual and religious structures encompass what truly resides within these different levels of existence? ... I'm hopeful that these reports will accelerate interest in the non-material realms, using whatever intellectual, intuitive, and technological tools we possess. Once there is enough interest in, and even demand for, information about them, such phenomena might become an acceptable topic for rational inquiry. Ironically, we may have to rely more upon science, especially the freewheeling fields of cosmology and theoretical physics, than on our more conservative religious traditions for satisfactory models and explanations of these "spirit-world" experiences. ... Therefore, I was neither intellectually nor emotionally prepared for the frequency with which contact with beings occurred in our studies, nor in the utterly bizarre nature of these experiences. Neither, it seemed, were many of the volunteers, even those who had smoked DMT previously. Also surprising were the common themes of what these beings were doing with so many of our volunteers: manipulating, communicating, showing, helping, questioning. It was definitely a two-way street."

- Rick Strassman, ***DMT: The Spirit Molecule***

At this point in the study Rick was steered towards the parallels between the experiences which his patients were reporting, and the accounts that were piling up of people claiming UFO abduction, and extraterrestrial contact. This was a field with which Rick had no prior knowledge, or even interest in. But he was becoming pushed to research and investigate, simply to try to find explanations for the anomalous, yet strangely heterodox nature of so many different reports. His discovery of the Psychiatrist *John Mack's* work became increasingly intriguing, when he began to see the similarities between the phenomena his volunteers were testifying to, and the people reporting alien abduction. To most of science such claims were obviously preposterous, simply the delusions of the lunatic fringe and unworthy of any serious attention. What Mach had uncovered was that there was certain aspects of these encounters that also had qualities of *altered states of consciousness*, with distortions of time and reality that often defined these alien encounters. Rick began to wonder whether it was possible that these experiences had been caused, or rather facilitated by natural bursts of endogenous DMT, and that these two phenomena might in fact be directly linked:

"I was not at all familiar with the alien abduction literature before beginning the DMT study. Neither were many of our volunteers. I knew almost nothing about it, and had little desire to learn more. It seemed much more "fringe" than even the study of psychedelic drugs! However, once we began hearing so many tales of entity encounters, I knew I could no longer plead ignorance of the wider phenomenon. Despite my better judgement, I now feel compelled to weigh in with my opinion regarding the experience of contact with "alien life-forms."

Let's review the popularly reported "alien abduction" experience. We will see the striking resemblance between these naturally occurring contacts and those reported in our DMT study. This remarkable overlap may ease our acceptance of my proposition that the alien abduction experience is made possible by excessive brain levels of DMT. This may occur spontaneously through any of the previously described conditions that activate pineal DMT formation. It also might take place when DMT levels rise from taking in the drug from outside, as in our studies."

- Rick Strassman, ***DMT: The Spirit Molecule***

There a number of ways these alternate realms of DMT can be experienced, and strangely a lot can depend on not only your individual mind set, but also factors such as open eye visuals, or closed eye visuals. At high doses, either way you will be almost certainly thrust into a totally new reality, which is usually extremely futuristic, with brightly coloured visuals with geometric planes of indescribable beauty, and which may be inhabited by non-human life-forms. Not only that, the beings are usually immediately aware of your presence, like you have trespassed on their territory and the security alarms have given you away. The main difference between closed eye and open eye visuals is that with closed eye, you often feel a sense of transportation - or a breaking through of a membrane that separates realities, which because of the speed, must be very close or parallel to us. With open eye visuals these realities can occasionally seem to not only coexist with us, but also interpenetrate the very space we live in. It can therefore seem possible to be in both dimensions at the same time, eerily superimposed through the material surroundings. These effects can sometimes be experienced during alien abduction experiences, and this can also add to the fear experienced. There is a sense that a rift in space-time has been created and can be subtly manipulated: there are striking features that the phenomenology of the two share:

"As the event begins, Mach says, "consciousness is disturbed by a bright light, humming sounds, bodily vibrations or paralysis ... or the appearance of one or more humanoid or even human-appearing strange beings in their environment." Mach emphasises the sense of high frequency vibrations many abductees report, which may cause them to feel they are coming apart at the molecular level. ... Despite the obviously unexpected and bizarre nature of what they are undergoing, there is no doubt in their minds that it is really happening. Thus, they describe their experiences as "more real than real." ... Some abductees feel there is some kind of neuropsychological reprogramming, or an enormously rapid transfer of information between the beings and experiencer. Aliens may communicate using a language of universal visual symbols rather than sounds or words. ... As Mach's work with his subjects progressed, he notes another common, perhaps even basic, element of the abduction experience. This is the transformational and spiritual nature of the encounter: "[t]he collapse of space/time perception, a sense of entering other dimensions of reality or universes ... a feeling of connection with all of creation." Abductees' sense of belonging in that realm may be so acute as to create a yearning for it - a desire "not to come back." Many abductees no longer feared death, knowing that their consciousness would survive the body's death. One even considered the idea of killing himself so that he could return to the blissful state he encountered during his abductions."

- Rick Strassman, ***DMT: The Spirit Molecule***

Another aspect of the data that was a powerful testimony to its reality, was that when people returned to these different dimensions they were sometimes greeted as a recognised visitor. There was often the sense that things had "moved on" from their last visit, and that time had progressed along without them, just as it does in our world, though not necessarily one of an *imagined* one. Some would even describe their interaction as a "relationship," and could also describe the distinct personality traits that characterised individual entities. These were not always friendly encounters, however, and the beings seemed to have their own autonomous motivations and roles. Sometim... was simply it seemed scientific curiosity, and even c... procedure. Occasionally their attitude was even malevolent anu and could provoke feelings of terror. Though these encounters we... usually idiosyncratic to each individual, there did seem to be some species genres that seemed to be more archetypal (such as insect mantises, reptilian, and even the famous humanoid greys). This does not establish the veracity of these entities, but it does make their possibility more compelling.

Eventually, in 1995 Rick wound down the study, partly because he felt that if he was maybe being a little reckless, exposing human beings to these profound and confounding experiences without having a solid scientific grasp and understanding as to what these experiences really were. Strassman is by all accounts not only a brave and professional seeker of the truth, but also a deeply ethical man. He was obviously uncomfortable with the potential ramifications of his research, and the possible psychological dangers it represented to his patients. He did, however, feel he had enough food for thought with this data to try to create his own model of brain function, and possibly how limited an understanding we really have of how consciousness operates. This would provoke him to question one of the most fundamental of all scientific assumptions:

"Most of us, including the most hard-nosed neuroscientists and non-materialist mystics, accept that the brain is a machine, the instrument of consciousness. It is a bodily organ made up of cells and tissues, proteins, fats, and carbohydrates. It processes raw sensory data delivered by the sense organs using electricity and chemicals.

If we accept the "receiver of reality" model for brain function, let's compare it to another receiver with which we're all familiar: the television. By making the analogy of the brain to the TV, it's possible to think of how altered states of consciousness, including the psychedelic ones brought about by DMT, relate to the brain as a sophisticated receiver. ... What happens when the spirit molecule pulls

...ne physical and emotional levels of awareness? ...ible realms, ones we cannot normally sense and ...an scarcely imagine. Even more surprising, these ...d. ... Returning to the TV analogy, these cases ...r than merely adjusting the brightness, contrast, and ...ious program, we have changed channel. No longer is the sho... watching everyday reality, Channel Normal.

DMT provides regular, repeated, and reliable access to "other" channels. The other planes of existence are always there. In fact, they are right here, transmitting all the time! But we cannot perceive them because we are not designed to do so; our hard-wiring keeps us tuned in to Channel Normal. It takes only a second or two - the few heartbeats the spirit molecule requires to make its way to the brain - to change the channel, to open our mind to these other planes of existence.

How might this happen?

I claim little understanding of the physics underlying theories of parallel universes and dark matter. What I do know, however, causes me to consider them possible places where DMT might lead us, once we have rushed past the personal."

- Rick Strassman, **DMT: The Spirit Molecule**

It is a testament to Rick's intellectual sincerity that when the trials delivered results that were not only contrary to his expectations and worldview, that he was prepared to rethink the entire way we conceive reality. He was reflective and creative enough to search for new models of thinking that could possibly explain the data he was receiving from his studies. His hypotheses that the brain may in fact be a *receiver* of consciousness, rather that its *generator*, is an incredible idea that may also be a paradigm that explains a diversity of other recorded and anomalous phenomena too, such as near-death and out-of-body experiences; subjects that science, within its current framework has no convincing answer for. The strange but solid science of quantum mechanics may also be pointing in this direction as well. The possibility that we are just one frequency of a multi-channel universe is now a distinct possibility, and one which science must surely investigate. Many of the current cosmological models that are currently being postulated include not just the existence of different dimensions within our universe, but also unfathomably large multiverses within a larger "metaverse" too. The possibility that similar parallel dimensions and planes of reality intersect ours is also considered:

"Parallel universes interact with each other when interference happens. There are, theoretically, an inconceivable large number of parallel universes, or "multiverses," each similar to this one and possessing the same laws of physics. Thus, there would not necessarily be anything especially odd or exotic about these different realms. However, what makes them parallel is that the particles composing them are located in different positions in each universe.
    DMT may allow our receiver brain to sense these multiverses."

- Rick Strassman, *The Spirit Molecule*

One man who was to arrive at similar conclusions, from a very different starting point, is the maverick but very knowledgeable historian *Graham Hancock*. Hancock is most famous for his very successful books positing the possible existence of an advanced civilisation which once existed in our ancient past, and one which was destroyed by a catastrophic rise in sea levels at the end of the last Ice Age. Though controversial, Hancock has amassed a huge body of data that supports this theory, and also has a wealth of encyclopedic knowledge of human history and culture. When he started a new project, looking at the deeper history of human evolution, he was struck by the incredible qualitative jumps that characterised certain periods of our cultural development. He realised that for thousands of years man seemed to make no technological or cultural progress at all, and that this time was essentially defined by the repetition of inherited customs, primitive technology and behaviour. There seemed to be very little change or progress during these periods. We seemed to be essentially conceptually stagnant throughout most of our history.

The first sign that man was developing new ideas and displayed creative intelligence, was in the incredible cultural leap of cave art, man's first pictorial attempts at imaginative symbolic representation. This also seemed to take place at similar times independently across the globe. This was to him the defining moment that has so far separated man from other animals, and was the beginning of human culture. As he researched and investigated this phenomenon (and Graham is always a meticulous and thorough investigator, no doubt a trait from his journalistic past), he realised that the symbolic imagery that was being depicted could only be really understood as the depiction of *altered states of consciousness*. This was by far the most convincing explanation for such features as geometric patterns and lattices, therianthropes (half-man half-animal hybrids), shamanic dissolution, and other phenomena that are commonly reported experiences of humans undergoing these altered forms of consciousness, but not experienced in everyday reality. He was very supportive of David Lewis-Williams' innovative neuropsychological interpretation of these ancient works of art, which had overturned years of academic consensus, and shook the foundations of the orthodox anthropological view of cave art as merely conceptual and imaginative renderings of real life. This view was extremely controversial at the time, and was bitterly and maliciously contested in ways that only professional academics seem capable. These theories though are now becoming internationally accepted as the most convincing theoretical model for interpreting this phenomenon. Graham explores these issues not only in great detail, but where possible always attempts to get a first hand look at the evidence (no matter how inaccessibly located some of these rare cave sites are).

This desire to understand at first-hand the subjects he was investigating pushed Graham to also experience these *altered states of consciousness* themselves, if he was to authentically gain insight into this shamanic model of pictorial art. Graham was to undertake a personal experience of the hallucinogens that are still used by traditional tribal shaman across the globe. These experiences included *ibogaine, ayahuasca, pure DMT* (which is smoked), and *psilocyc magic mushrooms*, and he gives a fascinating account of all these experiences, as well as a convincing expression of his own fears and amazement. Perhaps the oldest and most famous of these traditional psychedelics is the mixed plant brew of *ayahuasca*, and this was also the entheogen which most impressed Hancock. Not only was he astonished by the profound visual nature of the experience, but was also beguiled by the educative quality of the experience, which he found both nurturing, as well as forcefully exacting, and at times emotionally insightful. There have also been other biological benefits too, such as the physiological reduction of migraines he once suffered, a debilitating illness which had plagued him for much of his life.

These shamanic experiences have not only become an important and beneficial ritual in his life, they have also led him to question (like Strassman) our whole understanding of the ontology of reality. These "spirit realms" he has encountered have also led him to postulate that the entities experienced in these altered states, have possibly had a direct impact on mankind's psychological development and cultural evolution. Had they been mankind's covert guides and inspirers through man's history and pre-history? He was particularly struck by presence of therianthropes as cultural icons throughout so much of human folklore and ancient religions, beings only usually experienced in theses altered states. The very birthplace of human culture was the inception of cave art, which seemed to be a pictorial expression of the experiences encountered specifically within this context - with striking features still shared with *shamanic art* across the world today. And he wondered whether it was possible that these states set in motion the incredibly rapid dynamics of intellectual progress within art, science, mathematics, architecture and also the birth of our religions. It is in some ways a far more modern conception of the "stoned ape theory" elaborated by Terence McKenna, but one far more recent than he conjectured, and also one he would probably have been very intrigued by.

was also forced to question what were the fundamental of these experiences. The answer he was to find most ...ing was the same hypothesis with which Strassman was also a. ulating - that maybe the brain was not the *creator* of consciousness, but in fact simply *attuned* to it, and that the world was probably a thousand times more multidimensional than we currently realise: "I don't believe that consciousness is generated by the brain. I believe that the brain is more of a receiver of consciousness." He therefore theorised that there were many levels of existence that we were simply not biologically programmed to perceive in normal brain function, but could only be accessed under the specific conditions of altered brain chemistry, either endogenously through natural releases from the pineal, or exogenously through the physical ingestion of specific molecules. These realms might be around us all the time, but simply imperceivable and unnoticeable. Like Strassman, he pondered whether these alternate realities were comprised of the matter which we *know* theoretically exists, but have no notion *where* it is located:

"It may be that DMT makes us able to perceive what the physicists call "dark matter" - the 95 per cent of the universe's mass that is known to exist but that at present remains invisible to our senses and instruments."

- Graham Hancock, ***Supernatural***

To Graham, there was a also a distinct phenomenological difference between the two DMT experiences, that is between smoked N,N-DMT and DMT in the form of ayahuasca. This may be related to the much slower rate that DMT is metabolised by the body, or it may be related to the other chemicals that are often present in ayahuasca (such as 5 MeO DMT), but not present in pure smoked N,N-DMT. This is a widely reported phenomenon, it is also clear that the two experiences suit different personalities, depending on what the intention of the user is. Ayahuasca is often a far smoother, and gentler journey, and the realms that one visits are usually far more earthly and organic. These "spirit realms" are more related to natural and biological forms (with encounters with animal and human spirits reported far more frequently). Spiritual forms of snakes, crocodiles and even plants are also common, as well as the intuition that one is being "schooled" with information about how nature and the universe really function. There is often a more personal quality to the experience, and the perception that one is understanding the truth (both good and bad) about what we truly are and how we relate to other people. This can be either the most rewarding or traumatic aspect of the experience (occasionally both simultaneously). Because ayahuasca is metabolised much slower by the body, and lasts significantly longer (usually 4 - 6 hours) it is usually a gentler experience (though certainly not always). This can be a more nurturing, and occasionally loving spiritual encounter, though at times potentially very frightening as well.

Smoked N,N-DMT, however, is famous for being the "bungee jump" of psychedelics, and is often an overwhelmingly powerful trip, which can in a matter of seconds catapult one into a completely alien environment which is not only multidimensional, but also inhabited by non-human beings. This environment is not only hyper-futuristic, it seems to have features of almost impossible technological capability, but also it seems to be intensely informative - where an incredible amount of information is attemptedly being delivered (often in forms of mathematical symbols, and alien language) within a short amount of time. This communication is often perplexing and difficult to comprehend, especially in such a limited time-frame. Often the information is communicated in some form of telepathy, as if it is being in some way "downloaded." The duration of the event is usually over (even at full dose-capacity) within 10-15 minutes, and though this is a comparatively short experience, often the psychonaut can be relieved by this, because of the incredible intensity (and occasionally terrifying) nature of the experience. Though once over, one is often left with an intense sense of euphoria, wonder, joy, and sheer bafflement about what exactly just happened:

.ience with DMT was qualitatively different from the realms .igs ayahuasca introduced me to. For whereas the ayahuasca , seemed rich, luxurious, and abundant in transformations of organic and supernatural life, DMT brought me to a world - or some aspects of a world - that appeared from the outset to be *highly artificial, constructed, inorganic, and in essence technological.* ... Still, nothing that I personally encountered under ayahuasca was anything like the transparent geometrical space into which DMT projected me on the first of my two trips. With its sense of intelligent little entities scurrying around on printed circuit boards stuffing vast quantities of incomprehensible data into my brain, it had the impact of a technological array that had been created explicitly to give very rapid courses of instruction in complex information."

- Graham Hancock, ***Supernatural***

Hancock also reflected on where precisely the information that facilitated this experience was being drawn from. His favourite option was the receiver model of the brain, and that we were simply changing brain function to tune into these different channels that were broadcasting "all the time." There was, however, an alternate interpretation of this data, and that was that the pineal was in fact receiving and transcribing information directly from *DNA*. That is because we have recently scientifically verified that DNA is "bioluminescent," which means it *naturally emits light*. It is also known that we only understand a fraction of the total function of DNA, and that the vast majority of DNA is naively labelled "junk," because we still do not yet understand its full purpose. DNA is also known to be an incredible information storage system, so it is possible to encode an incredible amount of data on it. This supposedly "junk DNA" is known to have patterns within it, patterns that have the same form of syntax as a *language*. Some have postulated that these altered states are in fact the direct communication with information stored within DNA itself.

One of the most famous exponents of these ideas is the Swiss Canadian anthropologist *Jeremy Narby*. Narby is a committed anthropological field worker in the Peruvian Amazon, and spent many years researching the culture, customs and beliefs of the indigenous tribes like the Ashaninca, with a view to help preserve the traditional knowledge and ecological wisdom of these cultures. He became fascinated by their primitive, but highly sophisticated botanical knowledge, but when he inquired how they attained this information; he was more than a little perplexed by the answer that: "The plants told them." And assumed they were pulling his leg. Eventually they would trust him enough to offer him the means to access this "higher knowledge" of plant wisdom - through the ingestion of their traditional brew of ayahuasca. Whatever Narby's expectations were, they were utterly confounded when he was suddenly thrown into this "spirit realm" with talking snakes and other entities, and left with his scientific worldview reeling from the encounter. This event is vividly related in his most famous book:

"Speculating in this way, I realised that the hallucinations I had seen in Quirishari could also be described as three-dimensional images invisible to a normal gaze. According to my Ashaninca friends, it was precisely by reaching the hallucinatory state of consciousness that one crossed the impasse. For them, there was no fundamental contradiction between the practical reality of their life in the rainforest and the invisible and irrational world of the ayahuasqueros. On the contrary, it was by going back and forth between these two levels that one could bring back useful and verifiable knowledge that was otherwise unobtainable. This proved to me that it was possible to reconcile these apparently distinct worlds."

- Jeremy Narby, ***The Cosmic Serpent***

This was initially a huge cultural shock to him, but one that he was to become completely fascinated by. What also triggered his interest was some of the visual geometry of the visions he had witnessed, that to him as a scientist looked like representations of molecular biology. A science that would have been completely unknown to the indigenous tribes of the Amazon. The symbolic visual image of coiled snakes (a common entheogenic experience, and a cultural symbol which is iconic within many cultures across the world) reminded him of the double helix of DNA, and he wondered if this was in fact direct communication with molecular biology itself. He was also intrigued to learn that Francis Crick, one of the brilliant co-discoverers of DNA, had first glimpsed this structure while he was also in an altered state of consciousness himself, while using *LSD* (a fact he had kept hidden throughout much of his life). This seemed to Narby that there was some fundamental correlation between the hidden world of the "spirit realms," and the microscopically hidden world of molecular biology. This is also a possibility that Anthony Peake has explored in **The Infinite Mindfield**, that biophotonic light is what the *internal eye* of the pineal is actually decoding. Although this possibility is very plausible, one of the anomalies of this explanation is the fact that there is often some form of interaction with these "spirit realms," and human consciousness in these altered states. This is highly problematic if the experience is simply accessing *stored genetic information*, no matter how vast and sophisticated, and the communication is more of an interactive dialogue. Narby himself has postulated this problem, and alluded to the possible contradiction, even if the theory is beguiling in many other ways. The solution to its mystery therefore remains inconclusive:

"By using different techniques, it therefore seemed possible to induce neurological changes that allow one to pick up information from DNA. But from which DNA? At first I thought that I had found the answer when I learned that, in each human cell there is the equivalent of "the information contained in one thousand five hundred encyclopedia volumes" - in other words, the equivalent of a bookcase about ten yards long and two yards high. There, I thought, is the origin of knowledge.

On reflection, however, I saw that this was improbable. There was no reason why the human genome, no matter how vast, should contain information about the Amazonian plants necessary for the preparation of curare, for example. Furthermore, the ayahuasqueros said that the highly sophisticated sound-images that they saw and heard in their hallucinations were *interactive*, and that it was possible to communicate with them. These images could not originate from a static, or textual, set of information such as 1,500 encyclopedia volumes."

- Jeremy Narby, ***The Cosmic Serpent***

Narby, Hancock, Rogan, and Strassman were to all feature prominently within the best documentary on DMT so far made, the brilliantly executed ***DMT: The Spirit molecule*** by *Mitch Schultz*. The film not only features a veritable Who's Who of the N,N-DMT world, with just about every major figure connected to the subject represented. It also features incredibly beautiful graphic animations that seek to do justice to the astonishing, beautiful, bizarre, and alien phenomenology of the DMT experience. The project has also allowed access through their website (and through YouTube) to hours of unfeatured interviews and monologues which are of huge interest to anyone intrigued by this mystifying and haunting subject. This work was obviously a labour of love, and has done much to alert and educate the general public about this so far obscure and unexplained phenomenon.

What this film greatly signifies is that it is a vital field of interest to scientists, anthropologists, psychiatrists, artists, neuroscientists, mathematicians, and a subject that could have huge intellectual significance for not only our understanding of the manifold mysteries of the human mind, but also possibly our place in the universe (or possibly multiverse). ***DMT: The Spirit Molecule*** is not only an enthralling piece of filmmaking, it also manages to convey a real sense of the excitement and wonder of this topic, a wonder that has not diminished with the passage of time, or familiarity with the subject. Hopefully this work will inspire others to also marvel at its mystery, and help garner the conviction to further investigate and unlock its riddle, if we as a species are to evolve our understanding of its full implications:

"For millennia, mystics have essentially said that particles/matter exist instantaneously across space and time, but serve as a single layer of this deeply complex machine called life. And now, through scientific research, academia looks to be validating spiritual visionaries. The cultural significance of consciousness has skyrocketed in recent years, and our evolving technology remains one of the most dramatic driving forces for its re-emergence. ... It reshapes our perspectives of ourselves in ways we never imagined, and positions humanity at the cusp of the next step on the evolutionary ladder ..."

- Mitch Schultz, Foreword to ***The Infinite Mindfield***

V

"But once we have perceived the invalidity of this abstract infinite, and of the finite which is equally supposed to remain fixed by its side, this may be said about the emergence of the finite from the infinite, that the infinite passes out into the finitude just because, taken as abstract unity, it has in it neither validity nor permanence; and, conversely, the finite passes into the infinite for the same reason, because it is void. Or, rather, this should be said, that the infinite has ever passed out to finitude; that, absolutely, it does not exist, by itself and without having its Other in itself, any more that does Pure Being."

- G.W.F. Hegel, *Science of Logic*

Chapter 5

Alien Dimensions

Science and the Multiverse

"Sometimes the Star Maker flung off creations which were in effect groups of many linked universes, wholly distinct physical systems of very different kinds, yet related by the fact that the creatures lived their lives successively in universe after universe, assuming in each habitat an indigenous physical form, but bearing with them in their transmigration faint and easily misinterpreted memories of earlier existences. In another way also, this principle of transmigration was sometimes used. Even creations that were not thus systematically linked might contain creatures that mentally echoed in some vague but haunting manner the experience or the temperament of their counterparts in some other cosmos. ... In his maturity the Star Maker conceived many strange forms of time. For instance, some of the later creations were designed with two or more temporal dimensions, and the lives of the creatures were temporal sequences in one or other dimension of the temporal "area" or "volume." These beings experienced their cosmos in a very odd manner. Living for a brief period along one dimension, each perceived at every moment of its life a simultaneous vista which, though of course fragmentary and obscure, was actually a view of a whole unique "transverse" cosmical evolution in the other dimension. In some cases a creature had an active life in every temporal dimension of the cosmos. The divine skill which arranged the whole temporal "volume" in such a manner that all the infinite spontaneous acts of all the creatures should fit together to produce a coherent system of transverse evolutions far surpassed even the ingenuity of the earlier experiment in "pre-established harmony." ... In one inconceivably complex cosmos, whenever a creature was faced with several possible courses of action, it took them all, thereby creating many distinct temporal dimensions and distinct histories of the cosmos. Since in every evolutionary sequence of the cosmos there were very many creatures, and each was constantly faced with many possible courses, and the combinations of all their courses were innumerable, an infinity of distinct universes exfoliated from every moment of every temporal sequence in this cosmos."

- Olaf Stapledon, ***Star Maker***

The above quote is from one of the most incredible works of science-fiction ever penned, a phantastical travelogue through our universe, of alien planets and species, to intergalactic federations and civilisations, to the final encounter with the ineffable entity which was the author of everything that has ever existed. What makes the work so astonishing is that it was written in 1937, when science-fiction was still in its infancy. It still remains one of the most pioneering literary works to conceive of the complexity and multiplicity of alien life within our universe, and even dimensions beyond. The book is overflowing with rich imaginative conceptions of alien intelligence, perception, and psychology, and is one of the first books to render the idea of the "multiverse" in such a sophisticated literary manner. The term "multiverse" was first coined in 1895 by the psychologist and philosopher *William James*, in a somewhat different spiritual context, though the concept has existed within human culture in different religious, spiritual, and eventually even scientific forms for generations. The fundamental core of this concept is that there are realms of existence which are outside, or beyond our normal plane of reality, either in the form of different universes apart from our own: or possibly even coexisting alongside and "parallel" to it (some of these worlds are believed to interpenetrate and coexist with our reality). Whereas this was initially conceived in religious terms of "higher" and "lower" spiritual dimensions which the human mind, or soul, could travel (either through *dreams, altered states,* and *death*), they have now become the material for not only imaginative science-fiction - but also serious consideration within theoretical physics and modern cosmology.

There are a number of different models within cosmology that are currently being considered as hypothetical possibilities, often in response to understanding some of the unexplained phenomena which currently exists within our modern scientific worldview. Some of these models are purely speculative concepts, employed to articulate some of the almost philosophical concepts of modern science. Others have a purely mathematical basis, and are logical consequences of trying to unify different forces and fields, and to integrate differing theoretical constructs. All of them posit the conception that our universe might not be the only one, or that there are many different dimensions to reality that we might not usually be able to experience because of the limited biological nature of our modes of perception. Some of the most serious scientific models of these "multiverses" are:

1 *The infinite universe*: Our singular universe is in fact *infinite*, and therefore, if infinite, will include an infinite spectrum of different variations of the distribution of matter and life (including even identical versions of our planet and ourselves) within the fixed natural laws and conditions which govern our universe. These worlds will probably be too far beyond the "cosmological horizon" of our particular cosmic location to ever be scientifically verifiable (the speed of light condition will essentially limit the scale of our knowledge to the *observable* universe). This is also based upon the *cosmological principle* that there is nothing unique or special about our place within the universe, we are simply one element of an infinite spectrum of different possibilities, *all* of which would have to be realised in a true spatial infinity:

"In spatial terms, there is room in an infinite universe not only for everything possible to happen, but for an infinite number of infinite universes, in each of which anything possible can happen an infinite number of times. No wonder the Ancients recoiled from the idea, and preferred to imagine that the universe is finite and bounded by a celestial sphere. Aristotle, for example, was happy to consider the idea of infinity in mathematics, but said firmly in his *Physics*, that "there will not be an actual infinite." On the other hand, philosophers such as Aristotle were unhappy with the idea that the Universe might have had a beginning, because that would mean a beginning, and perhaps an end, to time. So they were willing to accept the idea of an infinite duration of the universe in time. This is almost exactly the opposite of the standard modern cosmological view of the visible Universe. Cosmologists today are quite happy to consider the idea that the Universe is infinite in space, but their standard models start from the Big Bang at a definite moment in time, 13.7 billion years ago."

- John Gribbin, *In Search of the Multiverse*

2 *Eternal inflation theory*: The eternal inflation theory (or *chaotic inflation* as is also known) posits the possibility that our own expanding bubble of a universe, is simply one pocket, or air bubble, within a foaming sea of alternate universes, all with very different natural physical laws, and all with random cosmological variations. Most would probably be utterly devoid of life (at least life as we conceive of it), and would all be created by the fluctuation of *quantum variables*. These have by chance produced the fine-tuned physical laws that compose our own universe with its "hospitable conditions" for the development of life. This theory was developed as a logical consequence of the inflationary models conceptualised for the Big Bang, and further pushed to their extreme conclusion within a broader cosmological framework. This model also spawns its own type of *infinities*, but these infinities are generated *outside* our local universe, and instead located in a never-ending generation of new universes, all comprised of different forms of cosmos with their own independent

existence. If the laws of physics are determined by quantum probability, then it is purely a case of mathematical chance as to how they will form and develop. Although this theory would be extremely difficult to verify, some cosmologists are studying factors such as the background radiation signature of the Big Bang, to see if there is evidence of any "cosmic collisions" with these other "bubble universes" as they could have left impact imprints that could be detected using our most advanced technologies:

"Within the framework of established knowledge of physics and cosmology, our universe could be one of many in a super-universe or multiverse. Linde (1990,1994) has proposed that a background space-time "foam" empty of matter and radiation will experience local quantum fluctuations in curvature, forming many bubbles of false vacuum that individually inflate into mini-universes with random characteristics. Each universe within the multiverse can have a different set of constants and physical laws. Some might have life of a form different from ours; others might have no life at all or something even more complex or so different we cannot even imagine it. Obviously we are in one of those universes with life."

- Victor J. Stenger, *Is the Universe fine-tuned for us?*

3 *The "many worlds" interpretation of quantum mechanics*: This is also known as the "*Hugh Everett interpretation,*" and is a model that was created and elucidated by the American physicist *Hugh Everett III*. This theory was conceived to eliminate the probability paradoxes that characterize the science of quantum physics, particularly the conception of reality as a collection of "probability waves" and the *collapsing of the wave function* by *consciousness* through the act of observation. His radical new model of the world leads to the conclusion that in fact *every possible event happens that can happen within reality* - with each version creating its own individual trajectory within its own particular universe. So the world that we currently inhabit is not the only one in existence, but one of an almost infinite variety. The physical reality

and individual conditions which have led us to choose one course of action over another simply bifurcates the world into different pathways, each one with its own unique and independent reality. In fact the universe has been doing this since its very inception at the Big Bang. This in essence obviates the paradoxes of the *Copenhagen Interpretation* of quantum physics that so perplexed Einstein: "God does not throw dice." was his caustic judgement. This hypothesis essentially cleaves the universe into an almost infinite multiplicity of different outcomes, one that is multiplying exponentially with each passing moment. Every interaction within time therefore generates its own unique world, with every spectrum of possibility physically embodied:

"To recap, initially quantum physics implied that the building blocks of matter, sub-atomic particles, are brought into existence by observation. If there is no act of observation then there is no matter. However, as we are all observers it is logical to conclude that we all create our own versions of reality, our own personal universes. Then Hugh Everett suggested that the Copenhagen Interpretation is correct, but physicists had misinterpreted the evidence and wrongly concluded that an observer brings about the collapse of the wave function. For him the probability wave doesn't exist because probability is not involved. In Everett's version of events there is not a one in six probability that a dice will fall giving a particular number but a one in one. The universe just splits into six copies of itself and in each universe a different number comes up. In trying to explain away a self-created universe, Everett has simply turned the egocentricity on its head. We all exist in our own universes not because we bring them into existence but because we all have our own private universes anyway. Not only that but there are literally trillions of versions of each of us all living all possible versions of our lives."

- Anthony Peake, *Is There Life After Death?*

4 *The simulated universe*: As the Oxford philosopher Nick Bostrom succinctly puts it: "There is a significant probability that you are living in [a] computer simulation. I mean this literally: if the simulation hypothesis is true, you exist in a virtual reality simulated in a computer built by some advanced civilisation. Your brain, too, is merely a part of that simulation." This is an idea that is gaining great currency, not just because of the commercial success of some popular science-fiction blockbusters, but also mathematically grounded in statistical probability. As our own versions of *virtual reality* become increasingly sophisticated, and with computer power growing exponentially every year, it is increasingly evident that soon such simulations will rapidly overtake the number of *authentic* universes that could actually exist. This rapidly multiplying figure of virtual worlds signifies that the likelihood of our own universe being an artificial construction is equally compelling. The possibility of verifying such a conclusion is itself fraught with problems, as we ourselves are simply part of the program itself, and our whole existence is simply encoded within the data processing capacity of a super-computer. It would therefore be impossible to *transcend* the nature of this situation anymore than a computer generated character could transcend its existence within our current technological simulacra. The only way we could really establish the *reality* of this situation would be to find "glitches" within the operating system of our universe, strange anomalies that could reveal possible *flaws* in the programme (a search some scientists are already undertaking in earnest):

"Even if we can't be sure whether the world about us is real or faked, we can at least contemplate the relative probabilities. How likely is it that the universe is a fake? The key point here is that fake universes are incomparably cheaper than real ones. ... Given these facts, it is clear that one super-civilisation inhabiting a real universe could at little cost simulate an almost limitless number of fake universes. In other words, the ratio of fake universes to real ones is likely to be enormous. If, then, a given sentient being cannot distinguish a simulation from reality, the vast majority of such beings are likely to be living in simulations. It follows that you and I are almost certainly simulated beings living in *The Matrix*."

- Paul Davies, ***The Goldilocks Enigma***

5   *The mathematical universe*: This is an idea that is currently being championed by the influential Swiss-American cosmologist *Max Tegmark*. Tegmark has accomplished many scientific achievements within his academic career, but is now most famous for his more controversial paradigm that all known mathematical structures correspond to some physical manifestation somewhere in the universe or "multiverse." Even if these structures are located inside dimensions that are outside of time and space. His theories are also known as the *Mathematical Universe Hypothesis*, and essentially postulates *everything that can exist, does exist*, which though at first may seem extravagant, is in fact surprisingly more simple an explanation as to why some things may exist and not others. His belief as a physicist is that mathematics is not just a mode of *defining* and *abstracting* the laws of nature, but more like the *fundamental essence* of nature and the world (including all conscious beings within it). It is also a form of mathematical *Monism*, in that it negates the existence of anything that is not a mathematical object. These complex mathematical forms could be located in dimensions that are far removed from the three-dimensionality that we are accustomed to in our ordinary reality - but instead theoretical constructs within the higher branches of mathematics:

"Now suppose that our physical world really is a mathematical structure, and that you are an SAS [self-aware substructure] within it. ... As a way out of this philosophical conundrum, I have suggested (Tegmark 1998) that complete mathematical democracy holds: that mathematical existence and physical existence are equivalent, so that *all* mathematical structures exist physically as well. This is the level IV multiverse. It can be viewed as a form of radical Platonism, asserting that the mathematical structures in Plato's *realm of ideas*, the

Mindscape of Rucker (1982), exist "out there" in a physical sense (Davies 1993), casting the so-called modal realism theory of David Lewis (1986) in mathematical terms akin to what Barrow (1991;1992) refers to as "in the sky." If this theory is correct, then since it has no free parameters, all properties of all parallel universes (including the subjective perceptions of SASs in them) could in principle be derived by an infinitely intelligent mathematician."

- Max Tegmark, **Parallel Universes**

6 *The organic universe*: This theory could also be termed the "*ecology of black holes*." This hypothesis has fairly recently aroused a lot of interest thanks to not only our increased knowledge of these enigmatic entities, but also our heightened understanding of their sublime importance within the cosmos. Once conceived in purely negative terms, as an irresistably destructive force that pitilessly consumes anything within its ambit, black holes are now also being reconsidered constructively (for example supermassive black holes are thought to be at the heart of all galaxies, and may be a crucial element in galaxy formation). Black holes in a magnitude of different sizes are now being linked to some of the most vital roles within sub-atomic activity and wider cosmology. It is now being considered that the infamous "singularity" that black holes are thought to contain at their core (where all the known laws of the physics break down), could in fact lead to *singularities* that also constitute the formation of *new universes*. Each singularity could in its turn create universes with similar constitutions to our own, and in turn become the progenitor of their own baby universes - a cycle that seems more comparable to biological evolution than atomic physics. Each singularity may itself contain within it stored information that could be similar to genetics and natural selection in the possible evolution of physical laws. Essentially the universes that succeed in propagating themselves, like species in the animal kingdom, will become the most successful and dominate this mutating cosmological family tree. This would lead to the most successful

physical variations at a cosmological level to evolve in a progressive manner, and the weaker cosmological combinations dying out:

"All the inhabitants of the original universe can see is a black hole, but the black hole is one end of a kind of umbilical cord linking the parent universe to a new baby universe. In the new universe, to any intelligent observers the other end of the umbilical cord appears as their own big bang, complete with inflation and the production of profuse amounts of matter and energy thanks to the negativity of gravity.

There is, of course, no need to stop at one bubble. New bubbles of spacetime can form wherever there are black holes in the original universe, and new bubbles of spacetime can form in the same way anywhere in any of the new universes, the babies that the original space has given birth to. The most profound implication of this insight is that our Universe may have been born in the same way, from the collapse of a black hole towards a singularity in another part of the Cosmic Landscape. Our Universe has to be seen as just one component in a vast (presumably infinite) array of universes connected by tunnels through spacetime."

- John Gribbin, ***In Search of the Multiverse***

7 *The string theory universe*: String theory has become one of the most central and also fashionable candidates for the *Grand Theory of Everything* (or TOE's as they are most frequently abbreviated to) of modern physics. It originally started off as a theory that explained the mathematical expressions of the collisions of high energy particles. But during the Eighties it was realised that they also represented possibly the most fundamental paradigm for understanding the underlying behaviour and composition of *all* particles. Instead of conceiving of elementary particles as tiny spheres or mathematical points, as in Newtonian mechanics, string theory posits the idea that particles are instead composed of tiny *vibrating strings* - whose "musical notes" corresponded to different particles (such as electrons, neutrons and photons). This revolutionary idea seemed to hold the key to

understanding all the particles and forces of nature within one cohesive package, and this generated huge excitement as to the possibility of unifying every physical field within modern physics into one *underlying form* (this is still essentially the Holy Grail of modern science, and still as yet its most elusive goal). These strings would be so infinitesimally small that they could hypothetically compose and describe even the most fundamental of particles: such as *quarks* that were inside the very nucleus of subatomic particles. They are therefore seen as the best candidate for finally unifying two of the greatest but independent theories of modern physics - *quantum theory* and the *general theory of relativity*. The main problem is, that there seemed to be not one, but a number of independent string theories, and they all seemed to mathematically require the existence of *ten different dimensions* (plus one of time) to cohere:

"The hope is that space and time will emerge from string theory as part of its description of reality, but this has not yet been achieved. You have to assume that space and time already exist to provide an arena for the strings to move in. But it's actually worse than that. In the simplest formulation of string theory, it is necessary to introduce extra dimensions of space. That is, our normal three dimensions of space have to be augmented by several others. Because we are not aware of the additional space dimensions, we have to invoke a mechanism to hide them - the process of *compactification*, ... In itself compactification of extra dimensions, although hard to visualise, is not a serious problem for the theory. A thornier issue is the fact that the shape and topology of the compactified dimensions are not unique. In fact, that is an understatement. Even a few extra dimensions can be compactified in a huge number of different shapes and topologies, and each arrangement leads to different particles and forces in the remaining (uncompactified) three-dimensional world. According to string theory, our world corresponds to just *one* such compactified shape. But which one? And what about all the others? What sort of worlds do they describe? As far as can be told, they would be very different from the world that we observe."

- Paul Davies, *The Goldilocks Enigma*

8 *The holographic universe*: The theory that our universe is in fact a *hologram*, a *projection* from another lower dimensional state is currently receiving great interest, and is the source of many scientific research experiments as well as mathematical conjecture. It is currently being married with *string theory*, with its other *dimensional* states, and is believed to be a model that could integrate quantum theory and gravity. This conception was seen as a way to explain some of the *entropy* and *information paradoxes* that haunted the physics of black holes, and seemed to describe quite accurately the mysterious activity of particles within black hole thermodynamics (with such activity as virtual particles on the event horizon that pop in and out of existence). This new conception has also developed to give more credence to *M-theory*, the idea that our universe exists like a dimensional *sheet* or *membrane*. There now seems to be statistical evidence that supports the string theory model of black hole entropy, which corresponds with the physics of a lower dimensional state with no gravity. So there is excitement that these models could be unified to produce a *quantum theory of gravity*. Probably the greatest pioneer of the *holographic universe*, however, must be the brilliant quantum physicist *David Bohm*, who as a truly radical and maverick thinker developed this new philosophical paradigm while scientifically unfashionable, and philosophically integrated these concepts to incorporate the intrinsic relationship of reality with *consciousness*:

"The more Bohm thought about it the more convinced he became that the universe actually employed holographic principles in its operations, *was itself a kind of giant, flowing hologram*, and this realization allowed him to crystallize all of his various insights into a sweeping and cohesive whole. ... One of Bohm's most startling assertions is that the tangible reality of our everyday lives is really a kind of illusion, like a holographic image. Underlying it is a deeper order of existence, a vast and more primary level of reality that gives birth to all the objects and appearances of our physical world in much the same way that a piece of holographic film gives birth to a hologram. Bohm call this deeper level of reality the *implicate* (which means "enfolded") order, and he refers to our own level of existence as the *explicate*, or unfolded, order.

He uses these terms because he sees the manifestation of all forms in the universe as the result of the countless enfoldings and unfoldings between these two orders. ... A piece of holographic film and the image it generates are also an example of an implicate and explicate order. The film is an implicate order because the image encoded in its interference patterns is a hidden totality enfolded throughout the whole. The hologram projected from the film is an explicate order because it represents the unfolded and perceptible version of the image."

- Michael Talbot, ***The Holographic Universe***

9 *The brane universe*: This was primarily the theory proposed by the brilliant theoretical physicist and mathematician *Ed Witten*, who came up with the extraordinary idea of *M-theory* (Ed has never disclosed what the "M" stands for, but many commentators have assumed that it stands for *Membrane*). Ed found a way of showing that all the different models of string theory could in fact be translated into each other. That in fact they were all describing different aspects or interpretations of the same thing. This was a bit like analysing the different physical forces which were in fact different facets of an underlying unity (such as electricity and magnetism being different forms of electromagnetism). His theory was that these different dimensions need not be compactified in the way conceived by most string theory models, but in fact spatially close, but at *right angles* to other dimensions of space. In this way our model of strings operating in a three-dimensional space might be misleading, when they are more like *vibrating strings* on a *two-dimensional plane* - or *Membrane*. These membranes (or two dimensional sheets) could in turn be flanked by a different sheet, or even a *multitude of different sheets*, all separated by

another dimension. Even this image could itself be misleading in that these *multi-dimensions* need not be considered as rigid or static in nature, but possibly in a far more dynamic and mobile relationship. Each brane could represent a different universe in its own right, and all be closely spatially bordered by these other different physical planes. It is even now being considered that Big Bang cosmology could in fact be the consequence of *brane-on-brane collisions*, and the huge kinetic inflationary models might be defined by the enormous energy transferals of these vast dimensional encounters:

"M-theory is the best candidate yet for the Theory of Everything. It also provides new insights into the search for the Multiverse, in more ways than one. The most obvious relates to the image of our entire Universe as a flat sheet of two-dimensional paper lying on a table, with an extra dimension at right angles to the surface of the paper, extending upwards in the third dimension. There is no reason why there couldn't be another sheet of paper on top of the first one, and another, and another - or a multitude of three-dimensional universes separated from one another in the eleventh dimension. This is quite a different concept from the idea of a multitude of bubble universes separated from one another by vast distances across three-dimensional space - the "universe next door" could be separated from us by only a tiny distance in the eleventh dimension ... But M-theory also suggests how different Big Bang universes might follow one another as a sequence in time, with one universe being born, Phoenix like, out of the ashes of a previous incarnation."

- John Gribbin, ***In Search of the Multiverse***

Dark Energy and Dark Matter: The question of different dimensions is not the only mystery that haunts modern physics and cosmology. Two of the most curious phenomenons which are considered so opaque they are both termed "dark" though they are probably distinct and unrelated. "*Dark energy*" is the mysterious force that is driving the expansion of our universe, though we currently have no explanation of it. This enigmatic entity was only recently discovered when cosmologists found a way to use distant supernovae as markers to discover if gravity was beginning to slow the expansion rate of the universe (and possibly produce the "big crunch" when it re-collapsed, and hypothetically reinflated in an endless cycle of creation and destruction). What was discovered shocked many physicists, some of whom even questioned the reliability of the scientific results as they were so counter-intuitive. The conclusion which was finally reached, was that instead of the expansion rate of the universe *slowing down*, it was in fact, *speeding up*. The mysterious force which was driving this process was subsequently labelled *dark energy* and seemed to function as some type of anti-gravity, not only fueling the expansion, but also *accelerating* it. This dark energy is currently estimated to be about sixty-eight per cent of the total energy of the universe - an extraordinary figure when we realise that we have only recently discovered its existence:

"That is, the universe is now expanding faster than before, and looks set to run away with itself if the trend continues. The discovery rocked the foundations of cosmological theory, built as it was on the firm conviction that gravitation acts as a brake on the expansion, serving to slow it down from its explosive start at the big bang to the relatively modest rate observed today. Now the name of the game has changed. A mysterious antigravity force is opposing gravity and has succeeded in transforming deceleration into acceleration."

- Paul Davies, ***The Goldilocks Enigma***

Dark matter is no less of a mystery, and it too has been a comparatively new discovery. In fact the only way we discovered its existence was through its *indirect effects*. We still have no understanding of what it is composed of, and what its relationship is with what we call "baryonic" matter (the visible matter that composes all the known physical objects of the universe). When physicists did their calculations on cosmic groupings such as galaxies and star clusters, as to their movements and patterns of rotation, it was realised that there was simply not enough matter, and therefore gravity, to hold these complex structures together within these formations. It was then recognised that the baryonic matter that we had believed represented all the visible mass of the universe was in fact only a fraction of the full spectrum of the total mass within the cosmos. Though there is much speculation, and intense research is being conducted into solving this mystery, as yet there is still no decisive understanding of either its composition - or even its relationship to the visible matter we do understand. All we do know is that it dwarfs this relationship in a manner that is still quite astonishing:

"In terms of density, the total amount of baryonic material in the Universe - the stuff stars, planets and people are made of - cannot be more than 4 per cent of the critical density. The rest of the matter known to exist from the way galaxies move, 23 per cent of the critical density, must therefore be in the form of some kind of dark matter which has not yet been identified on Earth. The search for this dark matter is one of the most pressing endeavours of particle physics today, but all we can say at present, and all that matters as far as this book is concerned, is that it exists, that it is spread very evenly through space, and that it is the gravity of dark matter that pulls baryonic matter (mostly hydrogen and helium) into gravitational potholes, where galaxies form like puddles in a badly maintained road."

- John Gribbin, ***In Search of the Multiverse***

The Religious Universe: The concept of the "multiverse" is fairly recent within scientific history, but it is not new to many of the ancient and world religions. Both *Buddhism* and *Hinduism* have furnished their belief systems with different worlds, spiritual dimensions, alternate universes, and planes of reality that are separate from our own. In fact Hinduism possesses numerous deities and almost innumerable universes, even if they are all inherently derived from the same divine source (*Brahman*). As *James Oroc* noted in ***Tryptamine Palace***, of all the world religions, Hinduism is the only one whose cosmology was even *close* to the real scale of the known universe. The three main

eligions, which are all essentially derived from the same
  assively underestimated the *true* picture of the cosmos
       r even science itself was astonished by the results of
     ver the past century, when the technology of modern
    omy furnished evidence of the universe's incredible vastness).
All three of the main monotheistic religions, however, had mystical wings that held a far more complicated and sophisticated form of creation knowledge, a knowledge that is believed to derive from sources far more ancient than their parent religions. These more unorthodox doctrines have often been denounced, and sometimes even persecuted by the hierarchical power structures of the mainstream churches, which often view them as aberrations and even heresies to their recognised canons of belief. These independent, but often familial doctrines are often labelled under the generic term of "*Mysticism*" and are based on a more direct and esoteric conception of the relationship of man and God. Their belief is grounded in the idea that man not only has the ability to have a direct and unmediated union with the *Divine*, but also that this capacity was at the *core* of all human beings:

"In mystic states we both become one with the Absolute and we become aware of our oneness. This is the everlasting and triumphant mystical tradition, hardly altered by the differences of clime or creed. In Hinduism, in Neoplatonism, in Sufism, in Christian mysticism, in Whitmanism, we find the same recurring note, so that there is about mystical utterances an eternal unanimity which ought to make a critic stop and think, and which bring it about that the mystical classics have, as been said, neither birthday nor native land."

- William James, ***The Varieties of Religious Experience***

1   *The Kabbalah universe*: The *Kabbalah* is a mystical branch of *Judaism*, a school of esoteric teachings which provides an ontological system and structure which is far more complex and refined than its orthodox mother religion. It is a form of mysticism which offers a comprehensive interpretation of the true nature of God: *Ein Sof* (no

end) and its relationship with humanity. It also possesses a rarified metaphysical cosmology of the spiritual and material realms, and their subtle interpenetrating connections. Its most famous and iconic symbol is the *Tree of Life* (or the *Ten Sephirot* as it is also termed), this tree is believed to visually and conceptually represent the forms of divine emanations of God's act of creation. Kabbalists also believe that it portrays the nature of divinity, man's spiritual ascent and pathway within it; as well as the fundamental essence of all reality.

The origins of the Kabbalah are sometimes contested, as well as its legitimacy within Judaism itself. Some schools see it as document of ancient wisdom and a complimentary guide to reading the *Torah*, whilst other more orthodox Jews view it heretically and suspiciously. It first came to global prominence within Medieval Europe around the Thirteenth century, as a school of mysticism which elaborated and supplemented Jewish philosophy (there are other non-denominational forms of the Kabbalah, either as syncretic religious hybrids, and even occult traditions), which have also aroused much interest and influence in modern culture too.

At the core of the Kabbalah doctrine, is the mystery and majesty of God (*Ein Sof*). In essence *Ein Sof* is formless, transcendent, and unknowable, as well as being limitless, boundless, and beyond human comprehension. This is God in his infinite purity. But God is also a being of *manifestation* too, and through this expression forms the subtle *ten theocentric* emanations with which the divine source constitutes the ontological structure of the universe. These are the *attributes* or *modes* which God defines and sustains the whole totality of existence. They are spiritual dimensions through which the Absolute expresses his will, and reveals his *purpose* within this act of creation. The *Ten Sefirot* are not just to be considered levels, or stages (often conceived in terms of light and its radiance) of illumination, they also correspond to man's own spiritual development and enlightenment. In this process it is not God who changes, but our own progressive understanding of Him:

" ... the Macrocosmos - Microcosmos, to which the emanated world is connected as the flux of light. Through further emanation the other spheres become the circles of the world, and this emanation is represented as a stream of light. Ten streams of light issue from the primal source, and these emanations, *Sefirot*, compose the pure world of *Azilut* (world of divine emanations), which is itself without variability; second, the world of *Briah* (world of creation), which is variable; third, the formed world of *Yetzirah* (the pure souls which are deposited in the material, the souls of the stars; the pure spirits are further differentiated as this enigmatic system proceeds); and fourth, the established world of *Asiah* (world of activation), which is the lowest vegetative and sentient world."

- G.W.F. Hegel, ***The Philosophy of History***

2   *The Sufi universe*: The Sufi religion can be at times contentious within Islam. Some of its followers expound that it is the *purest*, and most *spiritual flowering* within the religion. Other commentators contend it belongs more within a mystical tradition that predates all the major world religions, and is instead a part of the ancient family of groups devoted to the practise of divine *gnosis*. It has aroused opposition, and sometimes even suppression from some of the more worldly and political currents within the Islamic faith. The Sufi religion is rooted in a more *esoteric* and *experiential* knowledge of the reality of God, rather than the more fundamentalist interpretation of the divine texts as the main source of the literal will of Allah. The Sufis maintain that the key to understanding the divine is a direct inner-connection, it is a knowledge that is *felt* rather than *learnt*. The practical means of this initiation is usually achieved through a direct relationship with a spiritual master, or teacher, who will school his initiates over a number of years, and through this bond create a chain and direct lineage to the sacred origin of their beliefs. This relationship is to be one of love and purity, and the core of Sufism is the attainment of the cleansing of the mind from all worldly distractions which could prevent a direct union of the human will with that of God (through the purging the soul of any

base thoughts borne of the ego). In the words of Indian writer *Idries Shah*: "The union of the mind and intuition which brings about illumination, and the development which the Sufis seek, is based on love."

3   *The Gnostic universe*: Gnosticism is a derivation of Christianity, but has an extremely distinct ontology of the universe that is fundamentally at odds with orthodox Christianity. Their belief is that the *material world* is not the work of the *true* God, but in fact the creation of the *Demiurge*. The Demiurge is usually either perceived as an evil entity, who has fabricated this lower material world to deceive mankind, or in some cases as a demi-god, who has mistakenly assumed himself to be the real God, and his imperfect creation is simply the product of his illusions. The real God exists on another, higher dimensional, and eternal plane, which is perfect and beyond time and space. The material world is in essence an inferior and base *simulacrum* of the real divine kingdom, and the only way to access this true spiritual sphere is through *gnosis*, or *knowledge* at it is often translated. This knowledge includes the shunning of the material world, and often leads to an esthetic life of renunciation, voluntary poverty, sexual abstinence and personal philanthropy. The material world is in essence an illusion and a cage of the trapped soul.

This doctrine is philosophically radically dualistic: the spiritual realm is the divine plane, the source of everything good - the abode of light and purity and also the origin of the divine spark of consciousness which has been imprisoned in the degraded and corrupted world of matter. If the divine realm was characterised by purity and light, then the material realm was defined by impurity and darkness. There are many *Manicheanism* qualities within this religious conception of the struggle between light and darkness, of good and evil, and some *Mandaeanism* influence too. In Gnostic metaphysics, God is known as the *Monad*, or *Absolute*, the *One*, or *Bythos* (Depth and Profundity). The Absolute is the spiritual source of the *Pleroma*, and is the full manifestation of this divine realm of light. The various emanations from this divine source are known as *Aeons*, and there is a concentric cosmic structure to the *Pleroma* (or fullness), which is known to be the totality of God's Being or full Essence. This realm is one of goodness and perfection as well as being totally immaterial and ethereal. The world of matter and physicality is instead the domain of the Demiurge who is either malevolently deceiving mankind, or is a being who has mistaken himself for the real God, and his creation is simply a flawed and degraded reality which defines the limit of his powers.

To some radical sects within Gnosticism, Christianity was essentially worshipping the *wrong God*. Their belief was that the God of the Old Testament was not the true and pure God, but a jealous, vain, and wrathful entity, this was not the real God, but the Demiurge. Some of the sects within the Medieval French communities, such as the *Cathars* believed that this Demiurge was in fact *Satan*, or "Rex Mundi," the embodiment of evil, and creator and ruler of the physical world. The souls or spirits of the "fallen" were thereby endlessly re-incarnated here on Earth into other debased bodies until they could free themselves through *gnosis*. The only means of escape from this nightmarish situation was if this soul could enter a body that embraced *Catharism* as a lifestyle and revelation, and receive the Catharist sacrament: the *consolamentum* (consolation), and thereby escape the vile and polluted world of matter and return the soul to Heaven, its rightful home. This heresy would eventually lead to a direct confrontation with the Catholic church whose doctrines proclaimed the antithesis of such creeds, and eventually led to their bloody military suppression, which culminated in the genocidal *Albigensian Crusade*, and their virtual social annihilation:

"The Catharism of Montaillou was first and foremost a story, a myth. It was told over and over again, with variations, around the fire. To begin with there was the Fall. The Devil succeeded in leading astray some of the spirits surrounding the good God in Heaven. They fell from Heaven and were imprisoned here below by their seducer in vestures of earth, bodies of flesh, shaped in the clay of oblivion. These fallen souls sped madly from one deceased body to another, one vesture of decay into another."

- Emmanuel Le Roy Ladurie, ***Montaillou: The Promised Land of Error***

The modern Gnostic: One of the most famous modern Gnostics of the Twentieth century was unusually also a master of science-fiction. *Philip K. Dick* was to become one of the most celebrated writers of this genre in the world. His books and stories have been adapted into numerous Hollywood blockbusters: such as *Blade Runner*, *Total Recall*, *Next*, *Minority Report*, and a number of others. He spent most of his life, however, as a struggling novelist, as well as a short-story writer for science-fiction periodicals. He was just beginning to gain more financial security and critical success, when he died suddenly and unexpectedly, at the premature age of fifty-three. Philip K. Dick was a complex, and complicated man (he was married five times and had three children), and possessed an encyclopedic knowledge on a wide range of different subjects. His writing famously employed science-fiction as a medium to explore the subjects that fascinated him: these included *science*, *philosophy*, *theology*, *altered states*, *metaphysics*, *mysticism* and the nature of *time* and *consciousness*. His work is often viewed as a vehicle to illuminate many of the profound ideas which questioned the fundamental nature of time and reality, and our complex perception of it. He was also personally dogged by physical and mental troubles, but was later in life to experience two striking esoteric epiphanies which were to have a profound impact on his life and beliefs.

The first of these major "theophanies" was the watershed time of February-March-1974 (or *2-3-74* as he often termed it). This was a time when he experienced a number of profound hallucinations and altered states of consciousness, which compelled him to believe that he could possibly possess a split consciousness: one which existed in the present, and one located in an individual called "Thomas," a persecuted

Christian in the First century AD. He became increasingly drawn to the core concepts of Gnosticism, and questioned whether time and our perception of it might in fact be an illusion, a fabrication of the Demiurge to cunningly fool humanity, and blind it to its true nature. These themes are wittily explored within his last and posthumous books. Shortly before his death, he was to experience his second mystical "theophany," in which he encountered an entity which he believed was the true source of *all* reality and consciousness:

"I saw an infinite void, but it was not an abyss; it was the vault of heaven, with blue sky and wisps of white cloud (I am quoting from the notes I made that night). He was not some foreign God but the God of my fathers. I saw nothing, but I experienced his presence, his personality. And I was aware of him addressing me. ... Where I am, infinity is; where infinity is, there I am. I am everywhere and all roads, all lives, lead to me. Everyone will find me in the end. I revealed myself to you (in March 1974) and you saw that I am the infinite void."

Quoted from Anthony Peake, ***A Life of Philip K. Dick, The Man Who Remembered the Future***

VI

"In this enjoyment, then, that the orient "Light" of the world is discovered for what it truly is: Enjoyment is the Mystery of its being. For mysticism is not the concealment of a secret, or ignorance; it consists of the self knowing itself to be one with absolute Being, and in this latter, therefore becoming revealed. Only the self is revealed to the self; or what is manifest is so merely in the immediate certainty of itself."

- G.W.F. Hegel, *The Phenomenology of Mind*

Chapter 6

Home of the Absolute

5 MeO DMT and the Voyage to the Source

" ... I am next at the center of the universe, and I'm watching ... literally! ... and I'm watching all information that is known being sucked through a black hole *as data*, and it's coming from every direction at me. And it's wrapped up as data, and it's fucked ... it's like getting an adrenaline shot of *pure knowledge, absolute, complete,* and *meaning of life knowledge*, it's just ... BOOM! ... FUCK! ... and when I would try to respond to him, I'd see the thought that I am trying to say being written up as data, and that would split off into two, into four, into eight, into sixteen, into thirty-two. All the thoughts that went into creating the thoughts that I'm trying to make come out of my mouth, I'm watching ... It was the most intense... the only way I could describe the experience is imagine for a second, if you were a rat, just a regular rat, living a rat's life, with a rat's brain and a rat's consciousness, and all of a sudden, you smoked some shit out of a one-hitter with *Joe Rogan*, and you were infused with the consciousness that you have now, in that chair. But to realise that you are a rat, with your brain, you go: "Oh fuck!, I'm just a rat! I eat garbage, I'm only here to spread disease, and I'm fucking filthy." And you can't get rid of that knowledge. You go: "Oh fuck! Now I know I'm a fucking lower species." What are you gonna do? You gonna go back to writing *Man Show* monologues, going: "Oh fuck! I've been given, ... eaten the *Apple of Knowledge,* and now I'm trying to figure out a cable friendly euphemism for blow-job."

This is Doug Stanhope's (brilliant stand-up and militant atheist) account of the time he smoked 5 MeO DMT with friend and fellow comedian Joe Rogan. He would claim that it was the best drug he'd ever tried. Joe Rogan would also testify to the incredible power and the mind-blowing nature of the experience, and he even reflected that it was probably one of the most "humbling" lessons of his life.

5 MeO DMT is probably the most powerful psychedelic known to man (certainly according to its most enthusiastic users). And like N,N-DMT it is also endogenous to the human body. It is roughly four times the strength of N,N-DMT (that is it takes approximately a quarter of the amount to achieve a similar dose-requirement), which can be very dangerous if the two forms of DMT are ever confused, or sold under this category. The effects of the two chemicals are, however, distinctly different. Whereas N,N-DMT is famous for the unbelievably beautiful kaleidoscopic colours, and intensely visual nature of the experience, 5 MeO DMT is known to produce very little in the way of visuals (although sometimes fractalization and piercing bright light occurs), instead the experience has often been described as *"the Void."* To some this feeling is the ultimate entheogenic experience, and is "pure bliss," and to others the feeling is more like "pure terror." There seems to be very little middle ground at all with this chemical, either pure ecstasy or pure horror. The reason for the extreme polarity of this reaction - is that the experience is a launch into a *field of infinite consciousness*, and this field, and by extension we, are in fact all individual incarnations of the *Mind of God*.

5 MeO DMT is a complex tryptamine compound, and like its close cousin N,N-DMT, it is a natural brain neurotransmitter. It is also believed to be endogenously produced by the human organism in very much the same way as its cousin. It was first successfully synthesised in 1936, and is known to be a trace chemical in the traditional shamanic brew *ayahuasca* (5 MeO DMT is known to be present in small quantities in numerous plants, particularly in South America). It has

been used traditionally through the botanical ingredient of *Anadenanthera peregrina seeds* to create *Yopo snuff*, which is then insufflated: a practice that has continued for thousands of years by South American shaman. 5 MeO DMT is also famous for being a strongly represented constituent in the venom of the Colorado River Toad (*Bufo Alvarius*), and this has been exploited by some modern psychonauts as a source of this particular entheogen. This has led to the myth of "toad licking" within some media circles, as a way to ingest the psychoactive chemical, when in truth, the way to consume the compound, is to *dry* the venom (usually on glass), and then *smoke* it. It is also used as a sacrament by the *Temple of Awakening Divinity*, or to use its witty acronym, (T.O.A.D.) for short.

The most comprehensive and detailed work on 5 MeO DMT is a book called **Tryptamine Palace**, which was elegantly written by *James Oroc*. Oroc is a journalist and photographer (mainly in the field of extreme sports), and was born in the South Pacific nation of Aotearoa. Although he had some attraction to, and experience of hallucinogens and psychedelics in his youth, he would lose interest in the use of these substances, when other preoccupations and enthusiasms came into his life. It was only a chance encounter, many years later, when a recommendation of "a friend of a friend," aroused his curiosity. At first he thought that 5 MeO DMT was the fabled "McKenna DMT" that he had read about, but afterwards realised that 5 MeO DMT was in fact, quite a different beast. Even less was known or written about this compound than N,N-DMT; itself a rare and almost mythical creature. He was sufficiently intrigued to order some online (at a time when it was still legal), and give the experience a go, not sure exactly what to expect. He took a dose which he now realises was an extremely high one, and on the very limit of what could be considered "safe." Whether or not this may of helped him, because there was no way his body or mind could resist such a strong dosage, the power and impact of the full experience would leave him reeling, with his worldview and ontology in pieces. It was, he would later write, one of the most important and fundamental experiences of his life. Oroc was to succinctly explain his profound shock and utter amazement that his first encounter with 5 MeO DMT was to deliver him:

"From this very first experience, my view of reality was rearranged in a more comprehensive manner than I could have ever believed. I now consider 5 MeO DMT to be the only true entheogen I have ever encountered, since before that day I was a hardened atheist who embraced an inherited cynical scientific material-reductionist worldview, while now I inhabit a universe that is mystically inspired, and thus I'm indelibly aware of the existence of G/d. And it was this first 5 MeO DMT "experience" was solely responsible for radically changing me into a spiritually inspired, and much more hopeful, human being.

I can now state with unshakeable "faith" - a word that used to make my skin crawl - that I believe in the existence of the transcendent, formless Godhead and in the individual human ability to realize that transcendent ideal. I also now believe in the continued existence of my Soul (or consciousness if you prefer) after my physical body passes away - two newly acquired "leap-of-faith beliefs" - that have provided me with an enormous sense of peace and well-being, as well as a complete lack of fear of dying. The words of the great Russian novelist Vladimir Nabokov express my newfound perspective on the possibilities of the afterlife perfectly when he writes, "Life is a great surprise. I do not see why death should not be an even greater one."

- James Oroc, ***Tryptamine Palace***

Oroc was to spend much of the next six years researching, writing, and re-experiencing these altered states in a bid to provide answers to himself, and eventually the wider public, as to what he had encountered under its influence - as well as what its true significance might be. He would not only provide in his book some of the most profound and exquisite descriptions of this *"journey to the Source,"* ever related, he was to also offer some incisive models for the "scientific" basis for its underlying explanation. His conclusions were to parallel in many ways the scientific research into N,N-DMT pursued by Rick Strassman, and what it is possibly telling us about the nature of consciousness. The main point of departure seems to be that though Strassman considered the possibility that consciousness was in fact a non-local "wavelength" rather than a purely chemical epiphenomenon within the brain, he had not tied the physics of this model to any particular "energetic field." To Oroc, the true field of consciousness he experienced, and which pervades the whole of the universe - was intrinsically tied to the concept of the *zero-point field*, the primordial energetic substrate of all reality. The zero-point field is a scientifically recognised entity, and is like an invisible field of energy, composed of oscillating quanta of positive and negative electromagnetic waves and particles which are constantly coming in and out of existence. It is also known as the "quantum vacuum" (because physical space, even a total vacuum, is composed of these seething energy fluctuations of virtual particles emerging and annihilating each other). Whereas N,N-DMT seemed to alter the tuning function of brain chemistry to detect other "dimensional" frequencies, and hence the phenomena of parallel worlds and universes, 5 MeO DMT seemed to attune the mind to the underlying *source of all consciousness*, which he believes is located in the zero-point field, which itself permeates all of reality. This field, he believes, is the fundamental source of everything in the material world. His descriptions of this experience are worth quoting at length, not only for the illuminating beauty its exposition, but equally for its fundamental ontology of the nature of consciousness:

"There is no sense of time. I am somehow splitting, growing, spreading outward, and becoming a part of everything. I am pervading and connecting with the entire universe from within my very being. As I expand out and integrate into the happy multitudes and the universe beyond them, then my ego-identity begins to dissolve as the realization dawns that I am returning to the Source from where everything came. Looking around, in a dimension without time or space, I recognize everything and everyone as One, as the embodiment of all beings I have managed to love the most unconditionally. ... This infinite pulsating field of intelligent energy, from which all physical forms manifest and into which everything shall one day return, is the all-encompassing, brilliant bejeweled light of Love. The Godhead, the Supreme Mystery, the Conscious Infinity, the Pure Light, the Void that is a Plenum, Brahman, Yahweh - whatever you wish to call it. It is the Unnamable Name and the Creation Principle. I recognize It. I know that *It* is real, that I am part of It, and that in this moment I am able to return to It, like the Sufi "moth to a flame."

Resonating as one with my G/d and now having ceased to exist other than as a part of that divinity, all I have to do is breathe to feel the waves of omniscient energy radiate in and out of my ocean of bliss. My friends, my lovers, my life, my species, my world - we are all One and we are all part of G/d. *Atman* (individual consciousness) and *Brahman* (universal consciousness) are One. There is no way to differentiate between anything: I am lost in waves of an awestruck ecstasy that cannot be described, an egoless bliss. What Rudolf Otto called the *mysterium tremendum et fascinans* - the overpowering sense of awe that envelopes one who comes face-to-face with the Divine - is revealed within the singular realization of the true nature of my G/d: that G/d paradoxically resides both without and *within*."

- James Oroc, **Tryptamine Palace**

To Oroc, the claim by many psychedelics, whether they be natural like psilocybin mushrooms, or synthesised, like LSD, to be *entheogens*, was misleading, as entheogen specifically denotes an experience of *"the Divine within,"* and though these compounds are known to facilitate some spectacular altered states and experiences, they rarely (though occasionally) give the user a sense of a direct union with "God." This is, however, the specific phenomenology that is conveyed by those who ingest the high dose-requirement of this particular chemical. Some believe that it is *this* specific compound which is responsible for many of the "mystical states" that have been reported throughout history, the chemical road to the union of man and God (whether this was facilitated endogenously, through natural altered brain chemistry, or exogenously, through the chemical's consumption). And this state is achieved regardless of which (or any) world religion that the individual subscribes to, it is a universal experience unfettered by belief. There are many different names that denote this particular experience, such as *Samadhi, Nirvana, Satori* ... but the concept is essentially the same, that it is the fulfilment of the ultimate state of spiritual enlightenment. It is felt as the fullest form of self-realisation possible, and the ultimate apotheosis of the psychedelic experience. It is also characterised by a state of *non-dual being*, of a dissolution of the distinction of the self and the world, of subject and object, and the full union of all opposites. Another feature of the full experience is not only the intellectual awareness of this state of being, but equally a profoundly *emotional* one as well:

"As I let go I experience dissolution into an omniscient state of *Oneness*, a place where there is no difference between G/d, the physical universe, or me. We have ceased to exist as separate entities and now resonate as *One*. I resonate with the possession of a knowledge that radiates with the surest sense of Love - Love that is in everything, and *is* everything, and is so much more. It is a conscious Love more intelligent than anything we have ever known, a Love so great that it defies the need for a physical form and yet paradoxically realizes itself in us and in all creation. *Aum*. I become that Love and I know everything is *One*, everything is: G/d."

- James Oroc, ***Tryptamine Palace***

The whole phenomenon of this experience is not only shocking in its intensity, it only lasts, in comparison to many other psychedelics, quite a brief amount of time (certainly if you compare the experience to magic mushrooms, ayahuasca, or LSD). Though the full epiphany itself usually only lasts a number of minutes, this can vary a lot according to the dose and the psychological state of the consumer. Though *time* is an almost irrelevant concept when fully immersed within the experience.

Not only is the action-time of the compound extremely swift (literally seconds) after consumption, but as soon as the chemical is active within the brain, all notions of time and space rapidly become meaningless. Once within this other dimension, concepts of time, space, and identity can no longer take form or even make any sense, and so one can even feel that the few minutes within this state could just as well be an eternity. Others can also feel a strange sense of familiarity, that they recognise this place, and that have been there before.

One of the most impressive features of ***Tryptamine Palace*** is Oroc's detailed research and investigation into the scientific basis for such a phenomenon. His comprehensive search for the underlying mechanism, and a theoretical model that could explain the 5 MeO DMT experience, is one of the most beguiling qualities of the book. He takes us on a detailed trawl through the nebulous world of quantum physics, and explains how this science has revolutionised our model of the material world. He shows how it has supplanted the mechanistic (mainly Newtonian) and reductionist model of the universe in a way that a lot of orthodox scientists have still failed to fully comprehend. Many of the fields of science have not as yet fully assimilated the way that this science has demolished our concepts of material reality which had dominated for hundreds of years. And this has a huge bearing on our understanding of *consciousness* itself. He guides us on a tour of some of the most brilliant, and maverick, thinkers of our age, scientists who have fundamentally questioned what the notions of quantum physics could be revealing about our understanding of reality. In a way, many of these theoretical physicists are working in the terrain of classical philosophy, and confronting the whole epistemology of science itself. The ideas of outstanding thinkers such as *David Bohm*, and his "holomovement" are elucidated with insight, and probed for illumination as to what these theories might be telling us about the universe, its formation and its evolution:

"True reality is thus an infinitely multilayered, multidimensional wholeness, while what we typically consider "reality" is only a fragment of the whole. It is more like a dream or an illusion (or even a hallucination), from which our consciousness may one day presumably awake. ... According to David Bohm, matter is "condensed or frozen light." Therefore, the entire physical world can be regarded as ordered forms of slow-moving light. This includes organic life, whose existence and survival is entirely sustained by light energy from the sun. Life on this planet is a continuing process of light evolving itself into more complex forms of order: first into the simplest of atoms and molecules, then into increasingly complex forms of matter, then into exponentially more complex organic life forms (thanks to the wonders of DNA and RNA), and now - most recently, in our world at least - the latest evolution into conscious, questioning life forms."

- James Oroc, ***Tryptamine Palace***

Oroc's fascination and exposition of the fundamental core of quantum theory was to try to establish a theoretical basis for his own experiential knowledge. He was looking for a model of consciousness that could explain the nature of his own personal experience and how it was made possible. Here he was to find both support and inspiration from two of the most impressive writers on the *zero-point field* - *Bernard Haisch* and *Lynne McTaggart*. Two of the most important books that he was to encounter were Haisch's **The God Theory** and McTaggart's **The Field**. They were to both offer some fascinating and incisive observations that gave weight to these ideas about the nature of consciousness, and its possible relationship to the zero-point field. They also linked together the work of many scientists whose theories seemed to complement this striking new view. They too were attempting to find explanations for the phenomenon of consciousness, as well as the theoretical basis of "mystical states," (Haisch too is very sympathetic to the concepts of the "perennial philosophy") and other psychological phenomena and anomalies that science has not yet fully accounted for. Scientists such as *Hal Puthoff* whose pioneering theoretical physics were to offer a revolutionary new vision about the underlying structure of the universe, and how it functioned:

"A "mechanism" by which transpersonal coherence of this nature might be possible is suggested within Hal Puthoff's theories regarding the constant interaction of all subatomic matter within the zero-point field. He posits that the subatomic waves of the ZPF are constantly imprinting a record of the shape of everything through wave interference. As Lynne McTaggart explains it, when two waves collide, "each wave contains information, in the form of energy coding, about the other, including all the other information it contains. Interference patterns amount to a constant accumulation of information, and waves have a virtually infinite capacity for storage. ... As the harbinger and imprinter of all wave-lengths and all frequencies, the Zero Point Field is a kind of shadow of the universe for all time, a mirror image and record of everything that was."

If we consider the underlying structure of the universe to be "disturbances" caused by electromagnetic waves emitted by fluctuations in the zero-point field, then all possible permutations and information would be contained within the zero-point field (since it contains all possible waves). The amount of information that the zero-point field is calculated to be able to contain through the mechanism of wave-interference is virtually infinite, effectively making it the repository of all knowledge and the greatest "super-computer" imaginable."

- James Oroc, ***Tryptamine Palace***

This in turn led him to discover the work of the esteemed philosopher of science *Ervin Laszlo,* and his conception of the zero-point field as the underlying mechanism for the ancient concept of the *Akashic Record*. He too postulated that the zero-point field contained within it an imprint of all the information of every event that has ever taken place within the universe. That stored within it is the total library of all of existence as a permanent "informational field" which was also developmental. Oroc also considered the possibility that the effect 5 MeO DMT had on consciousness was to be able to chemically turn the brain into a "superconductor," a "Bose-Einstein condensate," a phenomenon that happens when under certain physical conditions, all atoms cohere together into the *same state*, and function as a *singular entity*. This was essentially an attunement of consciousness; so that resonated in *harmony* with this field, to a similar vibrational frequency. This would then be experienced as the *dissolution* of individual consciousness into the full totality of "Mind." This quantum coherence would in effect temporarily *synchronise* with the information from the zero-point field, or as Ervin Laszlo would famously define it: the *Akashic Field*. To Laszlo this field was the source of all material reality and consciousness, and that the self-development of the universe was predicated upon this informational entity. He believed that the purely random and directionless model of the universe (a model that still predominates in some scientific circles) was a profoundly mistaken perspective for accounting for the evolving complexity and coherence of a universe that had evolved biological entities whose consciousness could ponder its own existence. His was a profoundly more teleological conception of the forces that operate in our universe, or even multiverse:

"Which is to say that everything - the countless number of possible universes, the existence of every cosmological, chemical, quantum, and biological system, even consciousness itself - is G/d in-forming itself in an evolution towards G/d's realization. Every single Bose-Einstein condensate that has ever been formed through the interaction between wave and particle systems has imprinted itself on the "blank" plenum of the zero-point field, in the same way that the "blank" ground state of our own quantum consciousness is imprinted by our life's thoughts and experiences. The millions and billions and incalculable trillions of Bose-Einstein condensates of experience of this universe, and all the universes that have preceded it and all that will come after it, all act in coherence within the quantum, wave-like nature of the Akashic Field, so they become *One*."

- James Oroc, ***Tryptamine Palace***

This was a model that resonated powerfully with Oroc, and seemed to offer the most convincing theoretical model for his own experiences. A model that chimed authentically with what 5 MeO DMT had disclosed to him. He was also to investigate many of the world religions and spiritual teachers, to discover what they had to say about man's relationship towards this *transcendent* mode of consciousness, as well as what they could illuminate about the human condition. Oroc was to find great inspiration not only with the enlightenment traditions of many Eastern religions, primarily *Hindu* and *Buddhist*, but he was also sympathetic to the mystical traditions of all the major religions, and saw that there were elements of truth and beauty located in all of these forms. His concept of God, is in many ways comparable to the ideas of Aldous Huxley, and his non-denominational "perennial philosophy." This perennial philosophy is a completely non-sectarian embracing of all these different modalities of thought which are trying to articulate similar understandings - especially in their poetic, but probably impossible definement of the ineffable. To Oroc, no one religion has any monopoly of the truth, in fact, most organised religions tended to pollute the mystical source of these transcendent experiences, and instead rigidify and codify these beliefs into bone-hard orthodoxies, with their own hierarchies, and eventually all to earthly vested interests. This seemed to Oroc the antithesis of the transcendent experience, and the corruption of this divine knowledge which is not premised on any singular source of belief (Oroc was a pretty hardened atheist before his experience, God it seems loves an atheist just as much as the most devout believer). Instead all these different religious strands are best conceived of as elements of a much wider and richer tapestry:

"While I have mostly ignored the history of Christian mysticism throughout this book, it is important to mention that all over the planet there are on-going attempts by radical Christian groups to recover the core mystical precepts of early Christianity. I have also only briefly mentioned Islamic Sufism or the Jewish Kabbalah, two mystical movements that, like the Tibetan and Hindu esoteric traditions, are saturated with references to light and the twin ideas that both consciousness and God are primarily composed of light. Numerous further chapters could be written on the parallels in these traditions, but my knowledge of them is barely sufficient to scratch the surface. It is safe to say, however, that most mystical traditions share central concepts, such as the existence of God, the idea that our human consciousness is a part or reflection of God's consciousness, and of the primacy of light - rather than matter - in the universe, with the human soul/consciousness commonly being described in relation to that light."

- James Oroc, ***Tryptamine Palace***

Oroc was to also find that his experience also had a dramatic impact on how he viewed life on this planet, and a sense of the responsibility that his "awakening" had on his personality. He would gain a far greater sense of commitment to tackling social and environmental problems that face humanity. He would become far more sympathetic towards such schools of thought as "liberation theology." That the attainment of spiritual knowledge was to go hand in hand with some forms of social activism, and that social injustice and environmental degradation needed to be confronted if humanity was not to squander its precious gift of life. He saw there were many challenges ahead that modern society would have to face (such as population control, reckless squandering of natural resources, and huge social inequalities). It would also give him food for thought of how our materialist and market driven societies had eroded our capacities for spiritual growth, and how this is reflected in our relationship and treatment of our fellow human beings:

"The feeling of responsibility that I emerge from a 5 MeO DMT experience with is not a result of the awe induced ecstasy of the experience - it is an essential component of realization. I believe that charity and compassion are not necessarily natural to humans, they are higher graces, and as our societies have grown more and more complex, they have, correspondingly, only been earned by contemplation as the mature psyche "develops." This is a very difficult concept for the greedy materialistic modern mind to even consider, let alone try to understand.

Once considered "virtues," acts like charity and compassion are characterised as weaknesses in today's result-driven capitalist society. The philosopher Jacob Needleman has pointed out that although we are both material and spiritual beings, our culture has largely excluded the rich experience of the sacred from systematic awareness. Since we have much more tangible material experiences, we find it difficult to maintain a balance between the spiritual and the material. ... The result of the responsibility that is generated through a spiritual epiphany is expressed in contemplative activism. The Reverend George Cairns explains that, "The contemplative experience leads one to deeply understand that the inner work and the outer work are deeply intertwined."

- James Oroc, ***Tryptamine Palace***

Though Oroc has the highest respect for 5 MeO DMT as the ultimate entheogen, his book also has some cautionary tales within it, that urge people who wish to approach it to beware of the shear power of the experience, and to be extremely careful of the dose-requirements. He himself would face a couple of frightening episodes, when he was reckless and inattentive to the amount he consumed, and put himself in real peril. Not only his mind, but his body too. The most nightmarish account of such an experience was recorded by *Robert Augustus Masters*, and his casual ingestion of an extremely high dose in 1994 (in fact essentially the same amount that Oroc consumed on his first trip). Neither were prepared for the scale of the encounter, but whereas Oroc had to utterly surrender to the experience, Masters was horrified and appalled by what to him was this monstrously nightmarish vision of the universe. A nightmare he could not escape even when he returned to everyday reality; for months afterwards he was utterly traumatised by what he had witnessed. He became crippled by fear and despair and eventually required medical help:

"What I saw in front of me - the pipebowl, the faces of Marcelo and Nancy, the room, the framed sunlight, *everything* - immediately shrank into a rapidly contracting circle, as if it all were being viewed through the quickly closing aperture of a camera. In less than ten seconds, I became completely - *completely* - unconsciousness of waking/physical reality, finding myself bodiless in a horizonless horror that was madly and monstrously pulsating, moving far too fast, in all directions at once.

It resembled my ayahuasca journey at its most titanically wild and insane, sped up and intensified a hundredfold. I knew I was in serious trouble ... And *what* was *I* now? I was wide awake, but could not leave this domain, as I might leave a dream once I knew it was a dream. ... If what "I" was immersed in possessed any discernable or translatable form, it was vaguely reptilian, full of scaly-headed waves that were both surface and depth, both organic and metallic, sliding in and out of form. No limits, no edges, no exit. It was a timeless, boundless Chaos, continuously creating and consuming itself on every sort of scale with unimaginable power and ease and significance."

- Robert Augustus Masters, **Darkness Shining Wild**

Oroc was to write a separate *Appendix* and the end of his book titled: *Heaven and Hell - Potential Negative effects of 5 MeO DMT*, to investigate how the two of them were to have essentially similar journeys, but two completely different reactions. The main conclusion he drew, was that it was probably Masters' years of meditation and mental training that were in fact the *cause* of his anguish and "unabated horror." Because to try to resist the experience was a doomed enterprise, it could only lead to a greater depth of suffering. There was simply no way you could control this experience, and this was probably at the root of his terrible and traumatic reaction. Where Oroc was to find liberation and ecstasy within this absorption into the utter magnitude of the Divine, Masters would be repulsed by this "Cosmic Joke" which seemed to make a mockery of a person's identity, and disclosed that we were all simply trapped in this endless cycle of the universe "eating itself," an endless fate nobody escapes from:

"Everything was constantly dying and morphing into everything else in endless and impossible-to-anticipate ways, conveying to "me" with overpowering conviction that this was, and would *forever* be my - and our and everything else's - fate, beyond every possibility of form or individuation. Evolution without end. No exit - nothing existed apart from or outside this. I was in hyperterror, seeing without eyes, hearing without ears, desperately not wanting to die - or live - in such a condition."

- Robert Augustus Masters, **Darkness Shining Wild**

This is certainly not an experience that anyone should undergo lightly, as the consequences can be psychologically very serious indeed. However, if the person has the strength and faith to let go, the rewards can also be unimaginable:

"The best thing you can do at the height of the experience when your whole life seems to have come to that one unbelievable moment outside of space and time is to do *nothing* - and, if you can, just let yourself go. Let yourself dissolve. Rid yourself of "I" and go dance with the Supreme State of Being."

- James Oroc, **Tryptamine Palace**

The only other writer whose main literary subject is 5 MeO DMT is *Martin W. Ball*, who teaches Religious Studies and Native American Studies in Oregon, in the United States. Ball had studied Philosophy and Religious Studies as a student, and in which he qualified with a P.h.D. and a M.A. Ball is highly involved in the world of N,N-DMT, ayahuasca, 5 MeO DMT, and other entheogens, and has written and interviewed many of the leading lights in this field - including Rick Strassman, Jan Irvin, and James Oroc. He has also written a number of books on these subjects, as well as being fairly well acquainted with most forms of entheogen, their use, as well as their cultural context. Shortly after the publication (and podcast interview with Oroc) of

Tryptamine Palace, Ball was to have his own first *full blown* 5 MeO DMT experience, an event that would have a profound influence on his outlook and worldviews. Since then Ball has centered his writings (and podcasts) on what he believes the encounter has taught him, and his personal perspective on the true nature of reality. Ball has titled this view: *The Entheological Paradigm*, and uses this model as a prism for investigating what these conceptions can reveal about *God* and *being human*. To Ball the controlled (smoked) consumption of 5 MeO DMT is the best way for unlocking and understanding the true basis of the universe, and discover what lays behind the illusion of our perception of it:

"I like to think of it this way: What we experience as normal reality is God's altered state. In God's baseline state, all things are one and there is no separation. However, in ordinary reality, we experience things as separate all the time and most of us have no idea that we're actually God and all of what we experience is ourselves. In other words, when we humans are in our "normal state," we, as God, are fundamentally confused about the nature of existence. We are confusing all kinds of fantasies and illusions with reality and we think that there are a bunch of separate beings running around, all doing their thing. We are in God's altered state!

Conversely, when we alter our state of consciousness, we can get closer to the baseline state that is pure God consciousness. From my personal experience, this is best achieved through the ingestion of 5-MeO-DMT and is far more effective than any meditation regimen or other "mystical" practice. 5-MeO-DMT is about as altered as any human being can get, but from God's perspective, that state of consciousness is simply the way things actually are. In other words, that state of consciousness of complete mystical union is actually the super-mundane state of reality. It's the most ordinary, non-fantastical thing. It's the reality game that we're playing here in embodied form that is fantastical, given that it's all a complex and grand illusion."

- Martin. W. Ball., ***Being Human***

To Ball the real nature of our situation essentially makes most religious and metaphysical systems obsolete. To him religious doctrines are simply confused or misguided apprehensions of this core reality, and as such can only lead to greater mystification and a source of conflict. His belief is that our best method of comprehending our purpose, is to view our individual existence as simply different energetic incarnations of this one singular *Being*, without the necessity for different religious or spiritual ideologies. These he views as simply confusions, which are practically unhelpful in how we live our lives. In this sense it can be psychologically liberating to unclutter ourselves from a lot of the religious dogmas and beliefs that cloud our judgement and our perception of who we are. His hope is that we could probably experience a more authentic and happier life journey if we could just understand the surprisingly simple nature of our existences.

"Third, God is what we might call "the multi-being." God is one, but God has the ability to take multiple forms simultaneously, and thus is "the multi-being." The energy of life and consciousness that animates every living being in existence has its source in God, and actually is God in embodied form. Religions teach us that we have souls or spirits that give us life. This is fundamentally incorrect. Your life *is God*. You do not have a spirit or a soul whatsoever. You are God in a body. Any idea of a soul or spirit is superfluous, unnecessary, and ultimately incorrect. Every living being is God embodied directly from source."

- Martin. W. Ball, ***Being Human***

Equally Martin sees his conception of God in more of a scientific manner rather than in a religious fashion. God is basically a complex "energetic being" and our relationship can be similarly conveyed in terms of mathematical and physical manifestations of this primary energetic source. The whole universe is a vast field of different energetic forms, fields, and structures: from the most simple to the most complex. Biological evolution is therefore not only compatible with this model, it is simply the organic mechanism for the development of consciousness within these physical forms. The human species is then seen as basically "bio-vehicles" for God to travel around in, and have the capacity to experience its unique and individual existence in this particular "model." From the human perspective we are all separate and independent characters, but this perception of reality is essentially an illusion, that corresponds to the rules of the game which God has created:

"The key concept of the Entheological Paradigm is that of "energy." Everything that exists is a form of energy. While many religions and spiritual traditions make similar, if not identical claims, empirical, physical, and mathematical sciences have done a superior job in producing genuine, culture-free knowledge of reality and the true nature of energetic systems. ... While the Entheological Paradigm is largely in agreement with empirical, physical, and mathematical sciences, it is far more encompassing in its scope of energetic reality. Grand Unified Theories in physics, for example, has no account or explanation for the existence of life or consciousness in a supposedly purely "physical" system. The Entheological Paradigm is a true Grand Unified Theory for it accepts the unique energy of life and consciousness as not being a mysterious "by-product" of the universe, but rather as a fundamental energy of reality. In short, reality is itself a conscious, self-aware, living being. That being is God: The Unitary Energy Being. That being replicates itself in countless energetic forms simultaneously and is the very life and consciousness that finds expression in each individual living being. God is the very energy of existence and life itself.

God is a Fractal Energy Being that continually replicates itself through evolution within a universe of its own creation in order for there to be a genuine arena in which the exercise of free will, or conscious choice, by autonomous individuals, is an experiential reality."

- Martin. W. Ball, *The Entheological Paradigm*

One of the key problems to ever comprehending the truth to situation is the *ego*. The ego is a natural and essential component in any biological organism; in terms of defining itself as an individual being - not only in the daily challenge of its material survival, but also in terms of its self-development as a unique personality. However, the ego can also be a source of great anguish and suffering as well, when it totally controls the motivations and misconceptions a person can have about itself, and its situation in life. The ego can also be the most fundamental barrier to ever gaining a transcendent understanding of the true nature of reality:

"The ego is a self-referential program within the structure of *human consciousness*. The ego organizes its understanding of what is occurring to it within its energetic field (that which it experiences and senses through the construct of the body) as relationships between what it chooses to identify as its "self" and that which it chooses to identify as "other." The problem for the ego is that there is no inherent "self" within human consciousness. Therefore, in order for the ego to construct an identity, it must make what are realistically arbitrary decisions. If there isn't any *real energetic divide between the self and other (there is no fundamental "self" with which the ego can identify), then all such designations are by definition conventions and illusions.*"

- Martin. W. Ball, ***The Entheological Paradigm***

This function of the *ego* is also the most decisive barrier to ever having the *transcendent* realisation that can be facilitated by the altered states made possible by entheogens such as 5 MeO DMT. The most terrifying aspect of the experience is usually the process of the dissolution of *ego*: "you cannot take it along for the ride" in the words of Oroc. The resistance of the *ego* to this transcendent form of knowledge is to it a matter of *life and death*, and its horrified resistance is usually the most common factor for "bad trips" because the *ego* is fighting for its very *survival*. Only when a person is able to fully "let go" and completely

...the experience, is the ego dissolved and the truth of reality revealed.

The last word is probably best left to one of the most esteemed and experienced professionals working in the field of altered states of consciousness: *Stanislav Grof*. Grof is not only a trained psychiatrist and radical pioneer of transpersonal psychology, he has also supervised literally hundreds of psychedelic sessions. He has one of the most comprehensive and detailed understandings of altered states on the planet. He famously relates how the one time he smoked and insufflated 5 MeO DMT was probably the most powerful, and frightening entheogenic experience of his life, and forcefully relates this episode in his autobiographical book:

"The beginning of the experience was very sudden and dramatic. I was hit by a cosmic thunderbolt of immense power that instantly shattered and dissolved my everyday reality. I lost all contact with the surrounding world, which completely disappeared as if by magic. In the past, whenever I had taken a high dose of psychedelics, I liked to lie down and make myself comfortable. This time, any such concerns were irrelevant because I lost awareness of my body, as well as the environment. After the session, I was told that after taking a couple of drags, I sat there for several minutes like a sculpture, holding the pipe near my mouth. Christina and Paul had to take the pipe from my hand and put my body into a reclining position on the couch.

In all my previous sessions, I had always maintained basic orientation. I knew who I was, where I was, and why I was having unusual experiences. This time all this dissolved in a matter of seconds. The awareness of my everyday existence, my name, my whereabouts, and my life disappeared as if by magic. Stan Grof ... California ... United States ... planet Earth ... these concepts faintly echoed for a few moments like dream images on the far periphery of my consciousness and then faded away altogether. I tried hard to remind myself of the existence of the realities I used to know, but they suddenly did not make sense.

In all my previous psychedelic sessions there always had been some rich specific content. The experiences were related to my present lifetime - the story of my childhood, infancy, birth, and embryonal life - or to various themes from the transpersonal domain - my past life experiences, images from human history, archetypal visions of deities and demons, or visits to various mythological domains. This time, none of these dimensions even seemed to exist, let alone manifest. My only reality was a mass of radiant swirling energy of immense proportions that seemed to contain all existence in a condensed and entirely abstract form. I became Consciousness facing the Absolute.

It had the brightness of myriad suns, yet it was not on the same continuum with any light I knew from everyday life. It seemed to be pure consciousness, intelligence, and creative energy transcending all polarities. It was infinite and finite, divine and demonic, terrifying and ecstatic, creative and destructive - all that and much more. I had no concept, no categories for what I was witnessing. I could not maintain a sense of separate existence in the face of such a force. My ordinary identity was shattered and dissolved; I became one with the Source. In retrospect, I believe I must have experienced the Dharmakaya, the Primary Clear Light, which according to the *Tibetan Book of the Dead*, the *Bardo Thodol*, appears at the moment of our death. It bore some resemblance to what I encountered in my first LSD session, but it was much more overwhelming and completely extinguished any sense of my separate identity.

My encounter with the Absolute lasted approximately twenty minutes of clock-time, as measured by external observers. As far as I was concerned, during the entire duration of my experience, time ceased to exist and lost any meaning whatsoever. After what seemed like eternity, concrete dreamlike images and concepts began to form in my experiential field. I started intuiting fleeting images of a cosmos with galaxies, stars, and planets. Later, I gradually visualised a solar system and with it the Earth, with large continents.

Initially, these images were very distant and unreal, but as the experience continued, I started to feel that these realities might actually have objective existence. Gradually, this crystalised further into the images of the United States and California. The last to emerge was the sense of my everyday identity and awareness of my present life. ... My afterglow after this experience was unusually intense, profound, and long-lasting. I was able to work on the galleys of my book with extraordinary precision and capacity to concentrate. And yet, when I decided to take a break and closed my eyes, I was within seconds in a state of ecstatic rapture and experienced a sense of oneness with everything."

- Stanislav Grof, *When the Impossible Happens*

VII

"To explain what we mean by the neglect of the negative factor in thought, we may refer by way of illustration to the charges of Pantheism and Atheism brought against the doctrines of Spinoza. The absolute Substance of Spinoza certainly falls short of absolute spirit, and it is a right and proper requirement that God should be defined as absolute spirit. But when the definition in Spinoza is said to identify the world with God, and to confound God with nature and the finite world, it is implied that the finite world possesses a genuine actuality and affirmative reality. If this assumption be admitted, of course a union of God with the world renders God completely finite, and degrades Him to the bare finite and adventitious congeries of existence. But there are two objections to be noted. In the first place Spinoza does not define God as the unity of God and the world, but as the union of thought with extension, that is, the material world. And secondly, even if we accept this awkward popular statement as to this unity, it would still be true that the system was not Atheism but Acosmism, defining the world to be the appearance lacking in true reality."

- G.W. F. Hegel, ***Logic, Encyclopaedia of Philosophical Sciences***

Chapter 7

The Totality of Mind

The Akashic Field and the Pleroma

"What is implied by this proposal is that what we call empty space contains an immense background of energy, and that matter as we know it is a small, "quantised" wavelike excitation on the top of this background, rather like a tiny ripple on a vast sea. ... In this connection it may be said that space, which has so much energy, is *full* rather than empty. The two opposing notions of space as empty and space as full have indeed continually alternated with each other in the development of philosophical and physical ideas. Thus, in Ancient Greece, the School of Parmenides and Zeno held that space is a plenum. This view was opposed by Democritus, who was perhaps the first seriously to propose a world view that conceived of space as emptiness (i.e., the void) in which material particles (e.g., atoms) are free to move. Modern science has generally favoured this latter atomistic view, and yet, during the nineteenth century, the former view was seriously entertained, through the hypothesis of an *ether* that fills all space. Matter, thought of as consisting of special recurrent stable and separable forms in the ether (such as ripples or vortices), would be transmitted through this plenum as if the latter were empty. ... It is being suggested here, then, that what we perceive through the senses as empty space is actually the plenum, which is the ground for the existence of everything, including ourselves. The things that appear to our senses are derivative forms and their true meaning can be seen only when we consider the plenum, in which they are generated and sustained, and into which they must ultimately vanish.

This plenum is, however, no longer to be conceived through the idea of a simple material medium, such as an ether, which would be regarded as existing and moving only in a three-dimensional space. Rather, one is to begin with the holomovement, in which there is an immense "sea" of energy described earlier. This sea is to be understood in terms of a multidimensional implicate order, along the lines sketched in section 4, while the entire universe of matter as we generally observe it is to be treated as a comparatively small pattern of excitation. This excitation pattern is relatively autonomous and gives rise to approximately recurrent, stable and separable projections into a three-dimensional explicate order of manifestation, which is more or less equivalent to that of space as we commonly experience it."

- David Bohm, ***Wholeness and the Implicate Order***

David Bohm was one of the greatest quantum physicists of the Twentieth century, even if something of an unorthodox figure, he was a man far ahead of his time in many of his ideas and theories. His ideas of the *holographic* nature of reality are now gaining critical influence and credence within some of the current cosmological models involving brane and string theory. He was also far ahead of his time in postulating the possibly immense significance of the energetic substrate of the "quantum vacuum," otherwise known as the *zero-point field*. This quantum vacuum is essentially totally empty space at its lowest possible energy state; barren of any subatomic particles or matter in any form. This vacuum is now known *not* to be a complete "void" or totally *empty space* as previously imagined. It is instead, because of quantum fluctuations, full of fleeting and transient waves of electromagnetic energy which manifest and disappear in a perpetual dance of creation and destruction with itself. This is a dance of virtual particles and antiparticles, which are constantly flitting in and out of existence. For a long time physicists discounted the importance and significance of this field, believing that its influence was only negligible, as the energy within it was so low and finely balanced that it effectively cancelled itself out. It was therefore thought to be simply background noise to the physical manifestation of subatomic particles, or matter, which constituted the real building blocks of the universe. This conception is now being challenged by a number of scientists, philosophers, and researchers who believe that the significance of the zero-point field could be one of the most important and prescient subjects within science today.

One of these scientists is the German born American astrophysicist *Bernard Haisch*, who has developed his interest in the zero-point field *alongside* his more spiritual beliefs about the origin of the universe. Haisch was born in Stuttgart, just like the great German idealist philosopher *Hegel*, and like Hegel, his philosophy could be described as a form of *rational pantheism*, or even, in Haisch's case "scientific mysticism." This is a pantheism that does not reject the methods or findings of science, but rather embraces the advance of knowledge, and views scientific discovery as wholly compatible with a religious, or possibly more accurately, spiritual metaphysical worldview. His personal beliefs are also in sympathy with the "perennial philosophy" school of thought, which is an anti-sectarian form of mysticism which embraces many different forms of religious understanding, as well as different philosophical interpretations under this broad banner. His spiritual conception of the universe is chiefly informed by his knowledge, as an acclaimed astrophysicist, of the incredible fine-tuning of natural physical laws which have generated the cosmological evolution of our universe. And which have also facilitated the biological evolution of sentient creatures within it, who are able to question and conceptualise their reasons for existence. This "fine-tuning" is itself an astronomical feat of engineering, which poses the question that if our universe really is a product of random "quantum fluctuations," this would seem to imply that there either has to be an almost infinite spectrum of other physically diverse universes: all with completely different physical laws, the vast majority of which could not possibly produce life-forms in any way we can currently comprehend. Or there has to be some form of cosmic intelligence behind it, one which has generated and produced these specific conditions favourable to the emergence of life:

"It has come to light in the field of physics and astrophysics over the past two decades that there are numerous coincidences and fine-tunings of the laws of nature that altogether seem extraordinary unlikely and need to be explained. These key properties of the Universe have just the right values to make life possible. ... To be fair, it is possible to explain these coincidences and fine-tunings as just a matter of statistics. This involves a concept called the multiverse. The concept of the multiverse is that our apparently special universe is just one of a vast number of universes, all of which may be different from each other in unimaginable ways. There is no evidence whatsoever for this, but it makes an interesting theory. ... The problem is that you have to hypothesize a vast, perhaps infinite number of other universes. These hypothetical universes are ones we will never be able to detect because, being different, their laws of nature are incompatible with ours. That is required to make the statistical argument work. You need a huge, perhaps infinite sample. With a big enough sample the unlikely possibility - a Goldilocks's just right universe, like ours - becomes inevitable. ... As to how many other universes there must be for this kind of statistical solution to the Goldilocks mystery of the "just right" universe, the estimate ranges from 10 to the 500th power (again, one followed by 500 zeroes) to a literally infinite number. The "lower" estimate results from certain parameters in string theory, and therefore is liable to change (probably to a still higher value). It is, in any case, an unfathomably large number."

- Bernard Haisch, ***The Purpose-Guided Universe***

His views are premised on the fact that as our universe features these incredibly fine balances of powers, the factors of which only need to be changed by the slightest of degrees, to utterly transform the nature of our physical existences, a more simple explanation presents itself. That using the *Occam's Razor* methodology (of seeking the most basic and logical solution), isn't it far simpler to posit *one* universe, but one whose creation involved intelligent design, rather than an unfathomable infinity of other universes leading to this astronomically small chance result? He therefore contends that of the two scenarios which could explain this situation, which is the most *rational* and least *extravagant* conception? He proposes that as we have as yet no proof of the existence of these "other dimensions and universes," but we do have the testimony of *mystic experience* throughout the centuries, which have claimed some form of contact with this transcendent creative force. His belief is that this form of mystical experience, which is universal in its nature, and is the monopoly of no *one* religion, is a powerful testimony to its reality, and should not be dismissed as merely superstitious religious dogma. In fact, he views the doctrinal and *fundamentalist* interpretation of most organised religions (particularly the monotheistic ones) as divisive, if not pernicious. This dogmatic and literalist form of religious belief he sees as not only socially destructive and harmful, but in fact the *antithesis* of the truly *transcendent* nature of mystical experience. These mystical traditions have roots within all the world religions, and are open to access by any human being - irrespective of their faith or scientific worldviews:

"Brahman is said to be the sole reality, a transcendent intelligence beyond all attributes: unchanging, infinite, immanent; the Divine Ground of all matter, energy, time, space, being, and everything in this Universe and whatever others there may be. I equate Brahman with the Godhead in Christian mystical terminology, and Ein-Sof in Kabbalah. Godhead, Ein-Sof, and Brahman I thus take to be different names for the same infinite intelligence. Thomas Aquinas had a Latin name for the Godhead: Deus Absconditus, the hidden God. The appropriateness of "hidden" relative to a real and personal God the Creator will become clear. ... The Godhead is neither mind nor matter, but a reality beyond rational comprehension that is eternal, omniscient, omnipresent, and which experiences itself as pure consciousness and bliss. It is the Spirit immanent in everything that seemingly exists in the Universe, including us. There is no difference between the source and the manifestation. So how can we know this? Because in the Mystical Experience that people have, that is what is directly experienced and becomes known in a way and at a level that transcends language, logic, and rational knowledge.

Spiritual non-dualism, that our nature is ultimately identical with the transcendent consciousness behind all creation, is reported in the visions of all mystics. It is uniformly experienced by mystics from all religious traditions."

- Bernard Haisch, ***The Purpose-Guided Universe***

What Haisch is attempting to provide is a religious worldview which is in accord with scientific principles and understanding. The fundamental philosophical questions which have vexed thinkers throughout history are still with us, only now in slightly different and modified scientific forms. The underlying origins of cosmic creation still remain a mystery, as is its underlying metaphysical meaning. One of his most elegant scientific metaphors for the creation of the universe, which is also entirely compatible with esoteric spiritual ideas, is the "creation through subtraction" analogy. A metaphor which also resonates well with the mystics primary association of *light* as the most fundamental force in the universe, and *consciousness* itself as a form of illumination. This model implies that the real totality, the *infinite* which contains *everything* within it, is only made manifest through *limitation*. The transcendent, formless, infinite totality, only becomes actuality by negating elements of itself: in the same way pure white light contains the whole spectrum of colour within itself, but is only made manifest through the action of limitations which (like a prism) reveals its full properties. Infinite potential and possibility are transformed into *actuality* through this process of intelligent *subtraction*. This is a conception of the universe which mystics have attested to for aeons: that the infinite Godhead can only reveal itself through a process of *a filtration* of its essence - into the domains of time and space, and our material plane of reality through this transformative form of *reductive* creation. *Something* is not created from *nothing*; rather *everything* is reduced to *something* through the force of *negation*:

"The esoteric traditions tell us that creation by subtraction is one of the fundamental truths underlying reality. Put in terms that relate to the God Theory, these traditions teach that creation of the real (the manifest) involves subtraction from infinite potential.

Return for a minute to the slide projector. Turn it on without any slide inserted and project the pure white light onto the screen. That white light contains the potential to create every image you can imagine - your Thanksgiving family gathering, your trip to the Rockies, your high school graduation. Every one of those images, and an infinite number of others, are contained *in potentia* in the formless white light flowing from the bulb to the screen. All you have to do to project the picture you want is put in the slide that subtracts the proper colours in the proper places. The white light is thus the source of infinite possibility, and you create the desired image by intelligent subtraction, causing the real to emerge from the possible. *By limiting the infinitely possible, you create the finitely real.*

Let's take this optical metaphor one step further. The white light of a projector can convey more than just a static image. Project a series of images in rapid succession and you create motion. Although, on one level, that motion consists of a series of still shots, when those still shots are projected rapidly enough, the sum becomes greater than its parts. The resulting "motion picture" is more than just the sum of the images created out of the white light. People and actions and even emotions are made manifest by acting upon the formless white light in just the proper way; in just the right sequence. A replica of our real world can thus be created out of the unlimited potential of the white light through a process of intelligent subtraction carried out in space and time. A virtual reality is thus created out of the formless possibility. In fact, motion pictures are a concrete example of how a filter, the film, by selectively subtracting from the formless potential, can generate a virtual reality."

- Bernard Haisch, *The God Theory*

Haisch's philosophical temperament is also well suited for his professional and scientific study of the *zero-point field*. A study which has earned him much intellectual approbation and personal food for thought. Though his investigation of this enigmatic electromagnetic entity is primarily *scientific* in character (he considers that the zero-point field could be responsible for the force of *inertia* in matter, a revolutionary idea in physics), he also considers that it could be the source of almost *limitless energy* if properly harnessed. A power source which could have a massive impact on mankind's energy problems, and possibly a key to deep-space flight. His personal convictions also give him a novel perspective on this intriguing subject too. As this field itself does seem to display qualities of being an elemental residue from the original act of cosmic creation. A force which is at once intangible, but also permeating throughout all of existence, and therefore could possess some profound "spiritual" significance too. The esoteric traditions he admires all place light, rather than matter, as being the fundamental force within the universe, and in many ways he views the "quantum vacuum" like the faint background afterglow of energy suffusing through and *interconnecting* with everything. And this neglected field of study is still a mystery which is only just beginning to disclose its secrets:

"It is standard procedure in quantum theory to apply the Heisenberg Uncertainty Principle to electromagnetic waves, since electric and magnetic fields flowing through space oscillate as a pendulum does. According to that principle, at every possible frequency, there will be a tiny bit of electromagnetic jiggling going on. And if you add up all these ceaseless fluctuations, you get a background sea of light whose total energy is enormous. This is the electromagnetic zero-point field.

"Zero-point" refers to the fact that, even though the extent of this energy is huge, it is the lowest possible energy state. All other energy operates over and above the zero-point state. Take any volume of space and take away everything else - in other words, create a vacuum - and what you are left with is the zero-point field full of zero-point energy. We can imagine a true vacuum, devoid of everything, but in the real world, a quantum vacuum is permeated by the zero-point field with its ceaseless electromagnetic waves.

An old adage states that nature abhors a vacuum. Actually nature has nothing to abhor. The vacuum as a condition of complete emptiness, as an absolute void, does not exist. Rather the laws of quantum mechanics posit the seat of the zero-point field as a state of both paradox and possibility - a seething sea of particle pairs, energy fluctuations, and force perturbations popping in and out of existence. This state can support both quantum mischief and, I predict, veritable technological magic. It may represent an unlimited source of energy available everywhere, and perhaps even a way to modify gravity and inertia. The quantum vacuum is, therefore, in reality a plenum, but in keeping with tradition I will continue to use the term quantum vacuum.

The fact that the zero-point field is the lowest energy state makes it unobservable. We can only perceive it, as we perceive many things, by way of contrast. You eye works by letting light fall on a an otherwise-dark retina. But if your eye were filled with light, there would be no darkness to afford a contrast. The zero-point field has the same effect. It acts as a kind of blinding light that precludes our perceiving it through contrast. Since it is everywhere, inside and outside of us, permeating every atom in our bodies, we are effectively blind to its presence. The world of light that we do see is all the rest of the light that exists over and above the zero-point field."

- Bernard Haisch, **The God Theory**

The *zero-point field* is also absolutely central to the theories of *Ervin Laszlo* the (twice nominated for the Nobel Peace Prize) Hungarian system theorist and philosopher of science. Laszlo is by any standards a remarkable man; a gifted classical pianist, who played his first concert with the Budapest Symphony Orchestra at the precocious age of nine, he was to transform his direction and talents midlife, by dramatically undertaking a completely new vocation. His esteemed place as a musical performer was maintained until the birth of his first son, and afterwards replaced by a new career in the field of science (though his professional music life had always granted him enough free-time to also pursue his other private passion, the quest for *knowledge*). This transformation was partly facilitated by a chance encounter, and engaging discussion, with a stranger (who turned out to be a publisher), who was hugely impressed with the depth and breadth of his personal scientific research. This offer of publication in turn galvanised him to dedicate himself almost exclusively to the world of science, and the study of the underlying processes which shape all our existences. He has since become a highly qualified thinker and prolific writer, and has become one of the most distinguished and respected scientific figures in the world. These intellectual achievements are also bolstered by his involvement within a number of progressive international organisations as well. As his theoretical ideas matured and developed, the significance of the *quantum vacuum* became more and more central to his model of how the universe, and the laws of nature truly functioned. His conception of the *zero-point field* became central to how the informational forces within it generated the dynamic nature of cosmic progression. He was to name this informational entity the *Akashic Field*, based on the ancient Indian concept of the *Akashic Record*, which postulated the informational recording of every event which has ever happened in the universe in the form of a "cosmic memory bank." This is, to Laszlo, a reality actualised by the holographic storage mechanism of wave interference patterns within the zero-point field:

"We can specify how this information coding would work. We know that every moving object emits quanta of energy, and these quanta carry information on the objects that emitted them. The quanta form coherent waves that propagate in space, and - since space is not an empty domain but a complex field - the waves propagate in the unified field. The expanding wavefronts in the field interact and create specific patterns. These wave interference patterns are similar to the patterns created by interacting beams of light in ordinary holograms - they can be modeled by the same mathematics. This is important, for we know that in holograms the nodes of the interference patterns conserve information on the things and the processes that created the interfering light beams, or informed them between their emission and their reception. ... The Akashic field is a field of quantum holograms, a kind of superconducting cosmic medium. There is nothing in that field that could impede the frictionless spread and entanglement of the holograms that arise in it. The quantum holograms created by the waves emitted by the objects in space and time entangle throughout the field - that is, throughout space and time. They produce sequences of interference patterns, culminating in the superhologram that is the integration of all the other holograms. The superhologram carries information on all the things that exist, and have ever existed: it's the "hologram of the universe."

- Ervin Laszlo, ***The Akashic Experience***

Like Haisch, Laszlo was to view the "fine-tuning" of our universe as extremely unlikely to be the result of random bifurcating processes within a rudderless "infinite multiverse." Such an explanation is completely unsatisfying as a *coherent* scientific hypothesis to Laszlo. The incredible precision that is required in so many different atomic fields and forces, seem to signal an underlying intelligence at work; even if this intelligence is located within the *process* itself rather any external entity. Nature seems to betray some organising principle which is both progressive and functionally interconnected. The sophisticated developmental patterns which are suffused throughout the whole of nature, seem to belie the idea that it was either blind or directionless:

"Perhaps the most remarkable evidence for the coherence of the cosmos is the observed "fine-tuning" of its physical constants. The basic parameters of the universe have precisely the value that allows complex structures to arise. The fine-tuning in question involves upward of thirty factors and considerable accuracy. For example, if the expansion rate of the early universe had been one-billionth less than it was, the universe would have re-collapsed almost immediately; and if it had been one-billionth more, it would have flown apart so fast that it could produce only dilute, cold gases. A similarly small difference in the strength of the electromagnetic field relative to the gravitational field would have prevented the existence of hot and stable stars like the Sun, and hence the evolution of life on planets associated with these stars. Moreover, if the difference between the mass of the neutron and the proton were not precisely twice the mass of the electron, no substantial chemical reactions could take place, and if the electric charge of electrons and protons did not balance precisely, all configurations of matter would be unstable and the universe would consist of nothing more than radiation and a relatively uniform mixture of gases."

- Ervin Laszlo, *Science and the Akashic Field*

In Laszlo's cosmological model, it is the *zero-point field* which forms the basis of this cosmic memory function - and is not simply the irrelevant background noise to matter, but is itself the crucial organising force. This energetic substrate is a medium composed of electromagnetic waves, in which all information is imprinted in the same manner holographic images work: through coherent wave interference patterns. This energetic field does not only function in deep space - but is embedded through everything in the universe, including all matter and biological systems - including us. Every movement of every particle is thereby permanently imprinted onto this electromagnetic recording medium, and this functional form of cosmic memory is thereby able to learn and evolve towards a greater coherence. Cosmic evolution is not a random chaotic process, but instead a progressive and informationally *interactive* field. Our own universe is itself conceived as only one region of cosmological evolution within the context of a far wider Multiverse, of *Metaverse* as

Laszlo characterises it. The zero-point field not only carries within it all the information of our particular universe, but also all the universes that preceded it (and possibly all the ones to come). Our universe is itself interconnected to the wider cosmological family of other universes, which co-exist physically (or interdimensionally), and are to be viewed as an *ecology* of different cosmologies. And one that will no more cease as a process than organic evolution ceases through the loss of one particular species:

"Whether our universe expands and then contracts, expands infinitely, or reaches a steady state, the later stages of its evolution will wipe out the known forms of life.

This is a dismal picture, but it is not the whole picture. The whole picture is not limited to our own finite universe; there is also a temporally (whether or not also spatially) infinite or quasi-infinite Metaverse. And life in the Metaverse need not end with the devolution of local universes. While life in each local universe must end, it can evolve again in the universes that follow.

If evolution in each local universe starts with a clean slate, the evolution of life in local universes is a Sisyphean effort: it breaks down and starts again from scratch, time after time. But local universes are not subject to this ordeal. Each universe in-forms the vacuum in which it arose, and its in-formed vacuum in-forms the next universe. Thus in each universe life evolves more and more efficiently, and in equal times evolves further and further, toward coherence and complexity.

Cosmic evolution is a cyclical process with a learning curve. Each universe starts without life, evolves life when some planets become capable of supporting it, and wipes it out when planetary conditions pass beyond the life supporting stage. But the vacuum shared by all the universes is more and more in-formed, and it creates more and more favourable conditions for the evolution of life."

- Ervin Laszlo, ***Science and the Akashic Field***

If our "local universe" is itself interconnected or "entangled" to use the expression of quantum physicists, with a far wider Multiverse, or Metaverse, as Laszlo envisions it, then these informational fields must be in some ways informing each other in some method or form. As all these diverse cosmologies must themselves share the same processes of energetic evolution, as this seems to be its most fundamental nature. This conception seems to accord with David Bohm's portrayal of the universe as "ordered forms of light" evolving into more and more complex forms of energetic coherence. This could be the most primordial insight of the zero-point fields developmental modality of progression. Even if the laws of nature which characterise our particular "local" universe are also responsible for its eventual extinguishment, this will no doubt be itself reabsorbed and recycled by the larger Metaverse, in the continuous cycle of creation and destruction of energetic forms of physical manifestation. This is the *eternal* process of energy fields evolving and mutating into different, and *higher* forms of order:

"We have already seen how our universe and possibly myriad other universes in the Metaverse come into being, how they evolve and devolve, and how they give rise to the complex systems we call living. What do the stupendous processes tell us about the ultimate nature of reality?

The answer to this age-old question is now relatively straight-forward. *The most fundamental element of reality is the quantum vacuum, the energy- and in-formation-filled plenum that underlies, generates, and interacts with our universe, and with whatever universes may exist in the Metaverse.*

This answer corresponds to an ancient insight: that the universe we observe and inhabit is a product of the energy-sea that was there before there was anything there at all. Hindu and Chinese cosmologies have always maintained that the things and beings that exist in the world are a concretization or distillation of the basic energy of the cosmos, descending from its original source. The physical world is a reflection of energy vibrations from more subtle worlds that, in turn, are reflections of still more subtle energy fields. Creation, and all subsequent existence, is a progression downward and outward from the primordial source."

- Ervin Laszlo, *Science and the Akashic Field*

This cosmological model of informed evolution is not confined to the realm of interaction of subatomic particles, it is also the organising force within all biological processes too. In the same way that more crude models of Darwinian evolution were once seen as driven by the blind forces of genetic mutation, and chance adaptation, such a conception fails to account for the far more sophisticated patterns of a species development and its complex evolution and creative interaction with its environment. Blind mutation simply cannot account for the intricate genetic mechanisms which are often needed to make qualitative leaps throughout the whole functioning of the organism, rather than clumsy chaotic improvisations. Such genetic mechanisms need to be holistically encoded throughout the organism, for it to be able to function as an integrated whole. Such patterns of biological evolution seem to display an informational intelligence which is far beyond the capacities of random variability:

"Nevertheless, the basic mechanism of evolution described by Darwin was maintained unchanged. The "synthetic theory," the modern version of Darwinism, still insists that randomly produced genetic mutations and the chance fit of the mutants to the milieu evolve one species into another by producing new genes and the new developmental genetic pathways, coding new and viable organic structures, body parts, and organs.

However, random mutations are not likely to produce viable species. The "search space" of possible genetic arrangements within the genome is so enormous that random processes would take incomparably longer to produce new species than the time that was available for evolution on this planet. The probabilities are made a great deal worse by the consideration that many organisms, and many organs within organisms, are "irreducibly complex." A system is irreducibly complex, said the biologist Michael Behe, if its parts are interrelated in such a way that removing even one part destroys the function of the whole system. To mutate an irreducibly complex system into another viable system, every part has to be kept in a functional relationship with every other part throughout the entire transformation. Missing but a single part at a single step leads to a dead end. This level of constant precision is entirely unlikely to be achieved by random piecemeal modifications of the genetic pool."

- Ervin Laszlo, *Science and the Akashic Field*

Nor is this holographic process purely restricted to the atomic and biological fields. The processes of consciousness themselves are equally creating their own wave-fields of interference patterns which are being recorded in the informational records of the zero-point field. These vibrational frequencies are uniquely imprinting their activity within the quantum vacuum through the same mechanism of holographic resonance. This is a model of consciousness that has much resonance with the acclaimed psychiatrist and neurosurgeon *Karl Pribram* (who became a close working associate of David Bohm). As he was one of the first neuroscientists to postulate that the brain effectively functioned holographically, in the way that it processed the raw data of perceptual experience, and transformed it into memory (which tallied well with Bohm's theories that the universe itself functioned as a type of hologram). What this model of consciousness also suggested was that this process of informational relay and storage might not in fact be purely located within the organic structure of the brain, but was in fact being independently transfigured into the memory field of the zero-point field. So that in fact the whole body of a lifetime's memory is being permanently transcribed into the quantum vacuum through these subtle wave frequencies:

"This holds true for our body and brain as well. All we experience in our lifetime - all our perceptions, feelings, and thought processes - have cerebral functions associated with them. These functions have waveform equivalents, since our brain, like other things in space and time, creates information-carrying vortices - it "makes waves." The waves propagate in the vacuum and interfere with the waves created by the bodies and brains of other people, giving rise to complex holograms.

How do the body and the brain "make waves"? Physicists discovered that all things in the universe are constantly oscillating at different frequencies. These oscillations generate wavefields that radiate from the objects that produce them. When the wavefield emanating from one object encounters another object, a part of it is reflected from that object, and a part is absorbed by it. The object becomes energized and creates another wavefield that moves back toward the object that emitted the initial wavefield. The interference of the initial and the response wavefields creates an overall pattern, and this pattern is effectively a hologram. It carries information on the objects that created the wavefields."

- Ervin Laszlo, *Science and the Akashic Field*

This holographic energy field may also hold this information in the context of a nonlocal dimension, a dimension that has encoded within it all the pregnant possibilities for every future scenario. This could be in the form of an *Akashic Record* which already holds within it not only the details of everything which has already happened, but equally everything which will happen - or some form of possible interaction of events which are not yet actualised. This would be activated as a form of quantum interaction through the collapsing of the wave function from probabilistic indeterminacy to material actuality through conscious decision. This is a possibility explored by *Anthony Peake* as an explanation of how this Akashic Field could operate as an interactive interface with quantum probability. This could also account for certain anomalies that have surfaced throughout human history; of how certain forms of paranormal phenomena have been accessed through consciousness - and its relationship with this informational record, without resorting to a mechanistic determinacy of classical Newtonian physics:

"In other words all possible futures were encoded within the informational field right from the start. At each action the wave function of that potential universe is collapsed into an actuality that exists for a nanosecond before the next universe appears. From the first few nanoseconds of the Big Bang the universe has encoded all potential future states of its enclosed system. Like a huge computer hard drive the universe stores everything as a form of information that can be turned into a physical reality as each wave function collapses. In effect this means that information on everything that has happened and everything that can happen is encoded within this huge database. If this is the case then not only every actual future but also every potential future has an existence within this informational field. Within this informational field there is no time, just a permanent now in which everything exists as an informational potentiality."

- Anthony Peake, *The Infinite Mindfield*

This also raises the question of how consciousness functions and interfaces with these quantum forms of reality. One of the most beguiling models of how consciousness operates is based on the tiny microtubules which are suffused throughout the brain and are so small that they could be the biological mechanism of how consciousness interacts with material reality at the quantum level. There is currently a theory of "quantum consciousness" known as the *Orch-OR Model* which is being developed by acclaimed scientists Stuart Hamerhoff and Roger Penrose, and is explored in some detail in Peake's *The Infinite Mindfield*. This model postulates that it is the electrical activity within the neurons and dendrites which is at the heart of the informational relay between consciousness and quantum processes, and "the collapsing of the wave-function" in quantum reality. Microtubules have been found to be excellent conductors of electrical pulses, and it has also been discovered that there is a well established coherence and communication between the vast networks of microtubules throughout the brain. These could then act as waveguides for photons transporting these energy frequencies throughout the brain:

"Microtubules are obviously extremely small, so small in fact that quantum effects may influence how they function. In other words within the structure of microtubules the weird world of quantum physics spills over into the macro-universe that we exist within. Is consciousness therefore a quantum effect that manifests itself in the phenomenal world? This is what Penrose and Hamerhoff believe.

Each microtubule is a hollow cylinder with walls made up of a hexagonal lattice of the globular protein tubulin. This consists of a collection of large molecules known as polymers which are extremely stiff and strong. Bulges at the top and bottom of the tubulin structures are made of monomers, the single units that make a polymer. These are known as alpha and beta monomers respectively. Each monomer can have only two "confrontational" states. Each state has a different electric dipole. It is known that each monomer is affected by the dipoles of each neighbouring monomer. In this way they interact and in doing so they work like a quantum computer."

- Anthony Peake, ***The Infinite Mindfield***

This model also has some similar features to the brain function model which *Lynne McTaggart* articulates in her bestselling book ***The Field***. This work considers some of the vast implications of our understanding of the zero-point field, and looks at some of the most cutting edge neuroscience of the day and different specialists investigating this compelling area of consciousness research. It suggests a mechanism of *photonic transmission* of wave information which is carried through the hollow microtubules which can then act as "energy fields" which facilitate this form of quantum computing. There have been a number of research projects across the globe that support the theory that the brain makes use of quantum microprocesses, an idea which was once dismissed because of the warm temperatures of human biology. There have even been a number of mathematical models created which have added support to the physiological basis of these processes as a new model of brain function. What this model could also signify is a new way of understanding brain processing, on the one hand we have our brain holographically constructing the raw data of immediate perceptual experience, and imprinting this sensory information onto the electromagnetic patterns of the quantum vacuum, on the other hand this data can be retrieved through memory downloading this information from this very same field. The brain acting as the biological interface of quantum encryption and relay, the actual information is not located within the biological organ, but rather the mediator and transferer of this electromagnetic data:

"Others had theorized that the basis of all the brain's functions had to with the interaction between brain physiology and the Zero Point Field. An Italian physicist, Ezio Insinna of the Bioelectronics Research Association, in his own experimental work with microtubules, discovered that these structures had a signalling mechanism, thought to be associated with the transfer of electrons.

Eventually, many of these scientists, each of whom seemed to have one piece of the puzzle, decided to collaborate. Pribram, Yasue, Hameroff and Scott Hagan from the Department of Physics at McGill University assembled a collective theory about the nature of human consciousness. According to their theory, microtubules and the membranes of dendrites represented the Internet of the body. Every neuron of the brain could log on at the same time and speak to every other neuron simultaneously via the quantum processes within.

Microtubules helped to marshal discordant energy and create global coherence of the waves in the body - a process called "superradiance" - then allowed these coherent signals to pulse through the rest of the body. Once coherence was achieved, the photons could travel along the light pipes as if they were transparent, a phenomenon called "self-induced transparency." Photons can penetrate the core of the microtubule and communicate with other photons throughout the body, causing collective cooperation of subatomic particles throughout the brain. If this is the case, it would account for the unity of thought and consciousness - the fact that we don't think of loads of disparate things at once. ... All of this led to a heretical thought, which had already occurred to Fritz-Albert Popp. Consciousness was a global phenomenon that occurred everywhere in the body, and not simply in our brains. Consciousness, at its most basic, was coherent light."

- Lynne McTaggart, *The Field*

This is a very different conception of consciousness than that which is usually conceived by the material-reductionist model, which currently holds sway in the field of neuroscience, but is far more in sympathy with ideas envisaged by *Ed Mitchell*. Ed, the famous *Apollo* astronaut, while in space experienced an epiphany that consciousness was in fact a *singular field* to which every human was interconnected, rather than a process which everyone created in the isolation of their own biological neurochemistry. After this intellectual epiphany, when he returned to Earth he helped create and support a number of research projects and organisations to help explore and investigate the possible biological basis for this insight. He was to become one of the most pivotal figures in trying to fund scientific support and interest within this subject - which to him was experienced as an intuition, or flash of inspiration. If this field of information was in fact the true source of consciousness, a field which was "intrinsically connected" in the same way that subatomic particles could be universally interconnected and in a state of "quantum entanglement" with all other particles, then we would have to rethink everything we thought we knew about reality, and our means of perceiving it:

"Edgar Mitchell was one of the few to realize that, as a totality, their work presented itself as a unified theory of mind and matter - evidence of physicist David Bohm's vision of a world of "unbroken wholeness."

The universe was a vast dynamic cobweb of energy exchange, with a basic substructure containing all possible versions of all possible forms of matter. Nature was not blind and mechanistic, but open-ended, intelligent and purposeful, making use of a cohesive learning feedback process of information being fed back and forth between organisms and their environment. Its unifying mechanism was not a fortunate mistake but information which had been encoded and transmitted elsewhere at once. ... After Pribram's discoveries, a number of scientists, including systems theorist Ervin Laszlo, would go on to argue that the brain is simply the retrieval and read-out mechanism of the ultimate storage medium - The Field. Pribram's associates from Japan would hypothesize that what we think of as memory is simply a coherent emission of signals from the Zero Point Field, and that longer memories are a structured grouping of this wave information. ... If they are correct, our brain is not a storage medium but a receiving mechanism in every sense, and memory is simply a distant cousin of ordinary perception. The brain retrieves "old" information the same way it processes "new" information - through holographic transformation of wave interference patterns."

- Lynne McTaggart, ***The Field***

If this field of information is the most fundamental form of reality, which is in a perpetual state of "quantum entanglement" with everything else throughout the universe, then it is an informational entity very much like the formless, transcendent *Pleroma* articulated by the ancient *Gnostics*. The *Pleroma* is the timeless, spaceless, totality of God's powers, which permeates and informs all the dimensions of reality, and all levels of existence. It is everywhere and holistic, and constitutes the totality of the divine emanations, and interconnects everything within the universe (and possibly Metaverse). The Pleroma is a concept akin to the mystical traditions whose perception of God is at once intangible and transcendent, everything and nothing, but is in fact the ultimate reality; of which the realms of time and space are mere aspects and emanations, phenomenologies and manifestations:

"As we already know the Gnostics used the term Pleroma to describe this all-encompassing, timeless, totality. The literal translation of this word is "fullness" and it refers to the totality of everything that emanates from the mind of the Godhead. This defines perfectly the non-physical mega-universe of which the universe of matter is but one emanation. I would therefore like to suggest that this is the word we use to describe this universe of the mind.

The Pleroma is pure information, data encoded within a field that is reduced by consciousness to create physical reality seemingly external to itself. Of course this suggests some form of choice going on in that each point of self-awareness exists within an in-formational field of chosen data. As we have also discovered, writers such as Bernard Haisch and Martin W. Ball suggest that there is one singular consciousness that is the "in-formational field" itself. The Pleroma, for them, is the singular consciousness that experiences itself subjectively through the perceptions of each self-conscious entity."

- Anthony Peake, *The Infinite Mindfield*

In concluding, it may be of significance that one of the most common treatments within modern medicine is also still one of its most mysterious. And that has been the employment of anaesthetics to "knock out" patients while undergoing surgery, to help spare any psychological pain or trauma. The odd thing is, that science still does not have a full understanding of what is physiologically taking place in this common use of chemicals to "shut down the mind," and which seems to completely separate any conscious awareness from the biological body. This state is considered very different to many other brain states in which the body is disassociated from conscious awareness, such as sleep or hypnosis. It is more like the state of consciousness being completely *switched off*. One of the theories which has been proposed to explain this phenomena has also been linked to the role of microtubules as the real facilitators of consciousness. As the main chemical conductor within these incredibly small filaments is water, it has been hypothesised that the chemical carriers of these small electrical charges could be disrupted by any water discolouration (caused by anaesthetics) which could they disrupt and functionally block the reception of communication of microtubules and the zero-point field, effectively cutting of the reception of this signal and with it normal consciousness. If this is the case then it strengthens the theory that consciousness is not in fact *inside* the brain organ itself, but is instead located in a nonlocal dimension which exists apart from the physical realm. If this nonlocal realm where consciousness does preside can exist independently of corporeal matter, then it is theoretically possible that consciousness could indeed survive biological death. And this theory could also help provide a possible mechanism for *near-death* and *out-of-body experiences* which have been widely reported in modern times, as well as other forms of *altered states of consciousness*:

"Indeed one of the mysteries of anaesthetics is how the subject doesn't just lose consciousness but ceases to exist from their own viewpoint whilst under the effects of the anaesthetic. There is neither dreaming nor any sense of the passage of time. It is as if the very state of "being" is actually switched off. Could it be that without the in-formational inflow sentience is literally "switched off" in the same way a radio signal is not received when the receiver is similarly switched off? If this is the case then this presents strong evidence that the location of consciousness (if location has any real meaning within any quantum system) is not within the brain but is part of the zero-point field. Furthermore this suggests a model of consciousness in which self-awareness can exist outside of the body and, in turn, could survive the "death of the body."

- Anthony Peake, ***The Infinite Mindfield***

VIII

"And nothing serves better to shirk it than to adopt the conclusion that man knows nothing of God. To know what God as spirit is - to apprehend this accurately and distinctly in thoughts - requires careful and thorough speculation. It includes, in its forefront, the propositions: God is God only in so far as he knows himself: his self-knowledge is, further, a self-consciousness in man and man's *of* God, which proceeds to man's self-knowledge *in* God."

- G. W. F. Hegel, **Philosophy of Mind**

Chapter 8

To Death and Beyond

Near-Death Experience and the Multiverse

"I was there. I was on the other side." For a long time that was all I could say. I still get tears in my eyes thinking about the experience. Too much! It's simply too much for human words. The other dimension, I call it now, where there's no distinction between good and evil, and time and place don't exist. And an immense, intense pure love compared to which love in our human dimension pales into insignificance, a mere shadow of what it could be. It exposes the lie we live in our dimension. Our words, which are so limited, can't describe it. Everything I saw was suffused with an indescribable love. The knowledge and the messages going through me were so clear and pure. And I knew where I was: where there's no distinction between life and death. The frustration at not being able to put it into human words is immense.

I regret that words can't do my experience justice. I must admit that human language is woefully inadequate for conveying the full extent, the depth, and the other dimension I've seen. In fact, no pen can describe what I went through."

- Anonymous NDE experiencer, quoted from Pim van Lommel, ***Consciousness Beyond Life***

The field of *near-death studies* is a comparatively new phenomenon, even if the subject matter is probably as old as human history itself. Since the Seventies, with the publication of *Raymond Moody*'s bestselling book *Life after Life*, interest in this subject has skyrocketed, and also captured the public imagination. Now thanks to the internet, there are literally tens of thousands of reports of near-death experiences, with a number of websites devoted exclusively to this topic; as well as a number of scientific studies undertaken, and a literary field devoted solely to this area of study. It is now believed that there are literally millions of people who have had some form of near-death experience, though many of these are thought to keep this knowledge private, for fear of either intransigence or ridicule from their peers.

This is an area of research which has engrossed many in the scientific community as well. Various independent researchers and medical specialists have sought scientific explanation for this widespread, cross-cultural, pan-religious and completely *non-ideological* phenomenon. Not only are these experiences completely independent of a person's religious (or even non-religious) beliefs, they are also statistically independent of factors such as gender, age, disease, accident, or environment which triggered the circumstances of the NDE themselves. One of the most compelling qualities to the reaction to NDE's is the subsequent impact it seems to have on most people's perspectives on their lives. One of the most curious factors of people's relationship to this event is not only a heightened sense of *compassion* and sense of *spirituality* afterwards, but often a *weakening* of ideological religious beliefs, a testament to the truly universal quality of these experiences.

A number of neuroscientists have investigated the brain chemistry of these altered states of perception, looking for a cause for the phenomenon: they are usually searching for a materialist and scientific model for unlocking the biological basis of these experiences. There have been a number of hypotheses which have been put forward to explain such altered states, these include: The release of *endorphins* (pleasure inducing chemicals) released by a dying brain undergoing trauma, *oxygen starvation* (Anoxia) to brain function causing the widely reported "white light and tunnel" effect, *excessive carbon dioxide levels* (hypercarbic experiences), *endogenous DMT release* triggered during this specific biological crisis, and *temporal lobe seizures* causing profound hallucinations and chaotic neurological function. All of these factors have been researched, though none are able to give a convincing and definitive explanation of the near-death experience in all its unique and universal forms. The near-death experience usually comprises of a number of features, though not all elements will be present in all cases, but together represent a spectrum of its phenomenological forms. These include:

1 The *out-of-body experience*, the feeling of the separation of mind (or soul) and body.
2 The *tunnel experience*, the sensation of movement towards a beautiful bright light.
3 The *being of light*, greeted by a loving entity (sometimes a deceased family member).
4 The *life-review*, an often interactive three-dimensional playback of a person's life.
5 The *border*, the feeling of a demarcation line which defines another realm.

The first book which really identified these elements, and attracted wide public interest was *Raymond Moody*'s bestselling book **Life after Life**, and was to inspire many other researchers and writers to explore this enigmatic subject. Moody was the first to accumulate a body of independent testimonies, which seemed to offer supportive and corroborative evidence of the *shared* nature of many of their experiences - and challenge the current scientific paradigm for explaining them. Many of his case-reports were to provide moving and compelling accounts (often given through the protection of anonymity) whose individual integrity was also clearly apparent. Moody never attempted to claim that his research provided rigorous scientific proof of the survival of consciousness after biological death. He was always aware that such testimonies merely provided *experiential* evidence which our current scientific understanding could simply not account for, rather than conclusive and undeniable *facts*. These experiences were usually profoundly affecting, and sometimes even metaphysically challenging to the experiencers of the phenomenon, and this would often alter their subsequent lives:

"These remarks indicate why I refuse to draw any "conclusions" from my study and why I say that I am not trying to construct a proof of the ancient doctrine of the survival of bodily death. Yet I think that these reports of near-death experiences are very significant. What I want to do is find some middle way of interpreting them - a way which neither rejects these experiences on the basis that they do not constitute scientific proof nor sensationalizes them by resorting to vague emotional claims they "prove" that there is life after death.

At the same time, it seems to me to be an open possibility that our present inability to construct a "proof" may not represent a limitation imposed by the nature of the near-death experiences themselves. Perhaps it is instead a limitation of the currently accepted modes of scientific and logical thought. It may be that the perspectives of scientists and logicians of the future will be very different. (One must remember that historically logic and scientific methodology have not been fixed and static systems but growing, dynamic processes.)"

- Raymond A. Moody, **Life after Life**

Since the publication of his inspirational book, not only have the case-reports and public interest multiplied exponentially, science too has developed and advanced. The revolution in science which has been inaugurated by *quantum physics*, has been critical in facilitating the reevaluation of our understanding of consciousness, and its possible relation to brain function. At the core of this debate lies the still intractable and most mysterious question of consciousness, which is succinctly known as "the *hard problem*." Which is, what is the fundamental relationship of mind and matter? How does molecular matter give birth to the phenomenon of thought and self-awareness? Despite all of our increasingly sophisticated understanding of neuroscience and brain chemistry, this problem remains the proverbial "elephant in the room," with a growing body of evidence of the anomalies of consciousness which the materialist paradigm simply cannot explain. This is a debate which is not just confined to the question of the survival of consciousness after brain death, there are numerous other issues within psychiatry and neuroscience (for example the questions raised by *psychedelics* and even *savant* abilities) which highlight how profoundly limited our understanding of the totality of brain processing really is. There are now an increasing number of scientists and researchers who are willing to explore the theory of the *nonlocal* and "transmission hypothesis" model of consciousness which views the brain as an "interface," a *transceiver* and *transmitter* of consciousness, rather that its *producer*. Modern (quantum) physics itself points towards how crucial the role of consciousness is to the very existence and manifestation of material reality. This is a debate which *Chris Carter* eloquently explores in his detailed analysis of many of the scientific questions raised by the near-death experience:

"As for the objection that the transmission hypothesis is somehow fantastic, exactly the same objection can be raised against the production theory. In the case of the production of steam by a kettle, we have an easily understood model of alterations of molecular motion because the components that change are physically homogeneous with each other. But part of the reason the mind-body relationship has seemed so puzzling for so long is because mental and physical events seem so completely unlike each other. This radical difference in their natures makes it exceedingly difficult to conceptualize the relationship between the two in terms of anything of which we are familiar. It is partly for this reason that even though it has been more than a century since James delivered his lecture, in all that time neither psychology nor physiology has been able to produce any intelligible model of how biochemical processes could possibly be transformed into consciousness experience."

- Chris Carter, ***Science and the Near-Death Experience***

One of most obvious and glaring factors of the reports of NDEs, which appear to be fundamentally at odds with the brain-based explanations which have been proposed, is the *heightened* sense of perceptual experience which is so often attested to. Often these accounts describe the "ultrareal" nature of phenomenon, and how it is experienced as a profoundly *intense,* and perceptually *enhanced* form of consciousness compared to ordinary reality. The out-of-body experience (which is often the first form, or phase of a full NDE) have on numerous occasions provided testimonies of patients giving detailed accounts of operations, and of intricate medical procedures when they were deep in coma, or in cardiac arrest, when brain function was recorded as virtually *non-existent.* How is it possible for the malfunctioning brain to produce such coherent and often heightened awarenesses of reality at a time of profound trauma and biological degeneration? It would appear to be completely counter-intuitive to our understanding of complex brain processing. It is increasingly droll that our advanced medical knowledge of human biology, and sophisticated technological medical techniques, which have allowed us to rescue patients from profoundly serious medical crises (such as cardiac arrest and other once terminal conditions), would itself give rise to the increasing number of people who can recount such experiences which currently so baffles modern medicine. Are delusions and hallucinations created by a dying and misfiring brain undergoing extreme trauma, really capable of creating such widely and uniformly documented experiences of a spiritual and hyperdimensional reality which is far more authentic and enhanced than our own? This would seem totally contrary to all logic:

"The reports of enhanced mental processes and out-of-body perception of the environment at a time when we would expect brain processes to be severely impaired or entirely absent quite clearly seem to prove the production hypothesis false in favour of the rival view that the brain acts as a two-way receiver-transmitter, one that also restricts and filters out certain forms of consciousness and perception.

According to the materialists, these reports must be hallucinations somehow produced by a malfunctioning brain. Apart from the fact that we have found no plausible mechanism that can account for such hallucinations, the reports of accurate perception are simply inexplicable by this model."

- Chris Carter, *Science and the Near-Death Experience*

Probably the most comprehensive and detailed scientific book on the near-death experience is by *Pim van Lommel*, entitled **Consciousness Beyond Life**. Not only does he possess impeccable medical credentials as a world renowned *cardiologist*, he is also an exceptionally learned man in most fields of science. His detailed and scientific knowledge makes his book one of the most outstanding and comprehensive studies of the phenomena so far advanced. He, like Rick Strassman, are also impressive as human beings, in terms of their compassion, humility, and scientific integrity. His book is suffused with the empathy and respect which he obviously feels towards the individuals who have been brave enough to confide their experiences, and are to him, mentors rather than simply subjects of investigation. His example is a model to us all of how to absorb and process the profound information that is being revealed to us, and the implications that correlate to them. His conclusions are that consciousness is not an epiphenomenon simply created by the firings of neurons within complex brain chemistry, but rather a model which sees brain function as a *facilitator* of consciousness, which is itself located within a source which is independent of our biological existence, and instead derived from an energetic field which quantum physicists describe as *nonlocal*:

"The content of near-death experience suggests a continuity of consciousness that can be experienced independently of the body. But as I outlined above, identical experiences of an enhanced and nonlocal consciousness (sometimes coupled with contact with the consciousness of deceased persons) are reported during episodes of mortal fear, despair, isolation, meditation, on a deathbed, and during perimortem and postmortem experiences.

The questions still outnumber the answers, but in view of all the reported experiences of consciousness, we ought to seriously consider the possibility that death, like birth, may be a mere passing from one state of consciousness into another. Our vision of death is completely transformed by the near-inevitable conclusion that after physical death nonlocal consciousness can continue in another dimension in an invisible, immaterial world that encompasses past, present, and future.

Consciousness is not confined to the brain because consciousness is nonlocal, and our brain facilitates rather than produces our experience of consciousness. Whereas our waking consciousness has a biological basis, because our body functions as an interface, there is no biological basis for our endless and nonlocal consciousness, which has its roots in nonlocal space. Waking consciousness is experienced via the body, but endless consciousness does not reside in the brain."

- Pim van Lommel, **Consciousness Beyond Life**

Such a model would seem to give corroboration to the idea that this *nonlocal consciousness* is in fact located in a dimension which is significantly different to our own, in which our conceptions of linear time and causality do not function in the same way that our experience of it does in this particular physical realm. The vagaries of time and memory, and abilities such as instant recall, which are such rare attributes of most human beings, are not problems within these "higher dimensional realms" in which time and space are experienced in a more unified and interconnected form. Such a model is essentially grounded within a "permanent memory bank" of all of existence, which is in fact independent of all individual memory, posited as it usually is within transient and ephemeral biological mass of gelatinous brain matter. The famous "life-review" is a common feature of many NDEs in which a person's individual life is usually experienced in incredible detail, and in an incredibly short span of time (at least in an altered state of time perception) in a three-dimensional panoramic modality. Often they also get to experience any joy or suffering which they have inspired in other people, which afterwards leads them to become a far more kinder and empathetic person towards others they subsequently encounter in their journey through life:

"We learned earlier that during a life review every single detail of one's past life can be relived. Everything appears to be connected to everything else, an interconnection similar to what in quantum physics is called entanglement; everything is one. All past events appear to be stored and available as soon as one's mind turns to them. Time no longer plays a role; everything exists in an eternal present. This is true of time as well as place. NDErs report that during their experiences they can be anywhere in the past as soon as they think about or want to be in a particular place, be it as a baby in its crib, at a sporting event in elementary school, as a student on a study abroad program, or during a vacation in Australia. They instantly return to that situation and relive everything that mattered at that moment in time, including the emotional impact on themselves and others. The mind seems to contain everything at once in a timeless and placeless dimension. In quantum theory this timeless and placeless interconnectedness is called nonlocality ..."

- Pim van Lommel, ***Consciousness Beyond Life***

In this model of brain function, consciousness is not simply contained inside this organ, but is rather "attuned" to in the same way a television receiver is "attuned" to the radio waves contained in the wider energy field. In the same way that MRI brain imaging scans identify the sites of neuronal activity in complex thought processing, this could be instead viewed like the electrical activity within the circuits and transistors required for processing electromagnetically encoded information of the nonlocal signals dispersed throughout the wider energetic field. The programmes themselves are no more "located" inside the television than consciousness is purely "located" within the biological matter of the brain. This conception also offers a far more convincing explanation of the relationship between mind and matter, when it begins to provide a more coherent model for explaining a raft of other phenomena too (like the action of *psychedelics* on brain processing, *out-of-body experiences*, well as *mystical* and *religious* epiphanies, and possibly even "remote viewing" and other paraphysical claims). This model seems to provide a far more coherent and rational insight into the nature of near-death reports:

"According to this concept, our brain can be compared to a television set that receives information from electromagnetic fields and decodes it into sound and vision. Our brain can also be compared to a television camera, which converts sound and vision into electromagnetic waves, or encodes it. These electromagnetic waves contain the essence of all information for a TV program but are available to our senses only through a television camera and set. In this view, brain function can be seen as a transceiver; the brain does not produce but rather facilitates consciousness. And DMT or dimethyltryptamine, which is produced in the pineal gland, could play an important role in disturbing this process, as we saw earlier. Consciousness contains the seeds of all the information that is stored as wave functions in nonlocal space. It transmits information to the brain and via the brain receives information from the body and the senses. That consciousness affects both form and function of the brain and the body has been described in the discussion of neuroplasticity ("The mind can change the brain"). This view corresponds with what David Bohm has written: "Consciousness informs and in-forms."

- Pim van Lommel, ***Consciousness Beyond Life***

This concept is also harmonious with some of the theoretical models postulated about the zero-point field, string theory, and the holographic principle expounded by quantum physicists such as *David Bohm*. Central to this model is *Ervin Laszlo*'s conception of the zero-point field being the source of the *Akashic Record*, the underlying energy substrate of all reality. Here all information is encoded in this fields interaction with all subatomic matter, in which everything which has ever happened is forever imprinted as "interference waves."

Consciousness is itself embedded within this nonlocal field, and the brain is essentially the biological instrument, or *interface* with this informational totality; it is a two-way transfer mechanism for processing and storing all individual experiences. The zero-point field, is the real *medium* of consciousness, which is the reason that near-death experience is defined by its particular phenomenological forms. Consciousness is not extinguished through biological death - only this particular mechanism of communication has been terminated. Consciousness itself exists in another realm entirely, and so this extinction is perceived as a transition to a *higher realm* or *dimension* in which space and time no longer function within the same parameters as our plane of existence. This is usually experienced as a profound spiritual liberation, an escape in many ways from the physical constraints and limitations conditioned by our particular mode of living inside our material realm:

"Dutch Nobel laureate Gerard 't Hooft believes that the entire universe might be based on the holographic principle, a view he sees as compatible with string theory. In this theory the strings are one-dimensional oscillating lines (wave functions) floating in space-time. The idea of a holographic universe is based on an as-yet-unknown medium, believed to be strings or branes (this medium used to be known as the ether); in a nonlocal universe everything is encoded as wave functions in nonlocal space. Scientists now know that a vacuum is not empty; at absolute zero, -273.15 degrees Celsius, it is full of energy (a "plenum"), and at the subatomic level it undergoes constant quantum fluctuations that create new quanta "from nothing," which then immediately disappear again. What we see here is a kind of universal process of constant creation and annihilation. These quantum fluctuations are also known as the vacuum's zero-point energy. It can generate virtual particles (with antiparticles) that instantly destroy one another. The same pertains to the appearance and disappearance of virtual energy (waves). *Virtual* means that which is seemingly real or a possibility. There is general agreement about the (extremely short) existence of virtual particles and virtual waves (energy). In two recent and accessible books, ***The Connectivity Hypothesis*** and ***Science and the Akashic Field***, systems theorist Ervin Laszlo uses holographic field theory to argue that the universe is a fully interconnected holographic information field. His ideas are based on a theory of a zero-point field in the quantum vacuum or "cosmic plenum."

- Pim van Lommel, ***Consciousness Beyond Life***

This realm or dimension is usually experienced as an intensely *spiritual* plane which is suffused with a sense of unconditional love which is far beyond any Earthly human range of this emotion. It is in a purity of form which is felt as a direct connection of the real source and presence of the *Divine*: its fundamental site of origin. This presence seems intimately aware of the very essence of a person's unique personality and existence, and is forgiving and accepting of a person's flaws and imperfections. Such "mystical states" are not only accessible through the process of physical death, but can also be accessed through other forms of altered states (sometimes facilitated by brain neurochemistry granting access to these realms through endogenous or exogenous tryptamine release, sometimes through techniques of deep meditation or psychological epiphanies). These are often experienced as the dissolution of individual consciousness into a *non-dual*, or *universal* sense of consciousness, an indescribable oneness with everything that exists:

"All-encompassing consciousness is known by many different names. I call it endless or nonlocal consciousness. But it has also been called the higher or supreme consciousness, cosmic consciousness, divine consciousness, or the pure source or essence of our consciousness. Others prefer terms such as boundless consciousness, transpersonal consciousness, ultimate consciousness, unitary consciousness, or eternal consciousness, but all these terms refer to the same all-encompassing principle. Systems philosopher Ervin Laszlo calls this supreme form of consciousness the Akasha field because it stores all knowledge and an infinite amount of information. All of these different names refer to one and the same thing: there is an ultimate source of consciousness in a multidimensional space, and virtually every part of this endless and nonlocal consciousness is accessible to humans.

Forms of enhanced consciousness, coupled with a sense of disembodiment, are experienced under a range of different circumstances. The experience of this special state of enhanced or endless consciousness is totally different from normal waking consciousness, which is merely one element of nonlocal consciousness. Each aspect of our consciousness can be described as an aspect of endless or nonlocal consciousness, and the primary distinction between them is the intensity of the experience.

This endless consciousness can be experienced under different circumstances. In life-threatening situations we speak of near-death experience. But this term is far from ideal because enhanced consciousness can also be reported under circumstances that are not life-threatening. *Experience of insight* and *enlightenment experience* may be suitable terms as well as *religious* or *mystical experience*. But perhaps *experience of nonlocal or endless consciousness* is even better."

- Pim van Lommel, **Consciousness Beyond Life**

Probably the most incredible, and the most compelling near-death experience, is from an American *neurosurgeon, Dr Eben Alexander*, whose amazing book **Proof of Heaven** will probably be considered one the most iconic and comprehensive accounts of consciousness beyond life so far attested to. What makes this book so fascinating is not only the personal and autobiographical elements within it (themselves quite moving and interlocked), but also the idiosyncratic nature of his extremely rare form of illness; the detailed medical supervision of it, which was undertaken at the very hospital where he was employed. In these almost unique circumstances he was able to get access to the precise details of his physical and neurological states while in his week long coma, an illness he was not thought likely to survive, let alone make a full recovery.

The key event happened in November 2008, when he was suddenly struck down by a mysterious illness, collapsed, and was rushed to the nearest medical center, the *Lynchburg General Hospital*. Here he was treated by some of his own work colleagues, who quickly became anxious about the obvious severity of his condition. He was finally diagnosed with an *extremely* rare form of *bacterial meningitis*, and when his spinal fluid was checked it was full of pus. By this time he was already deep in coma, where he was to remain for the next seven days. Despite his treatment with massive doses of antibiotics, there was no real patient response. Days later, to the devastation of close family and friends (especially his children), it was acknowledged that there was very little hope (possibly one or two per cent) of him surviving, and even if he did, the destruction undergone through the brutal conditions of his illness would probably leave him brain-damaged for life. As the family and hospital were contemplating the unthinkable, the withdrawal of medical treatment, suddenly, as if by a miracle, he returned to consciousness. Despite a few days of extreme confusion and paranoia, as his brain rebooted to reality, he was then able to relate his incredible story. An experience that would turn most of his beliefs upside-down, and utterly transform the way he perceived the world. His son (also a trainee neurosurgeon) was to give him the best advice he ever received, and told him not to read any *near-death literature* until he had transcribed all of his memories of what he encountered, so no influence or bias could interfere with his testimony. When he had finished relating his tale he would then begin to research not only the burgeoning body of near-death literature, but also the new scientific paradigms which were being developed in quantum physics and consciousness research. He was *astonished*. He realised that despite all of his years as a practicing neurosurgeon, as a peer reviewed medical specialist, and highly educated academic, that he in fact knew very little about *consciousness* itself. He of course "knew" that consciousness was generated by the brain, that it was a chemical epiphenomenon located in the complex chemical firing of neurons located in this gelatinous body. He also "knew" that consciousness could not survive the biological demise of this organ; and that the existence of a personal and

loving God was extremely unlikely, given the adv
knowledge we have accumulated about the physical s
universe within the paradigm of materialist science in
fields. That was until he had his near-death experience in
coma.

In his bestselling book, he chronicles the whole phenomenology of his experience, a period when his brain was brutally attacked through this aggressive illness, and was shown by scans to be virtually inactive, and unresponsive, with the neo-cortex (which mediates all the higher functions of consciousness) utterly shut down. As a neurosurgeon, he would have concluded that he should have no awareness, or memory of this time at all. His brain would have been completely unable to create a coherent form of consciousness, let alone a *heightened* one. But this was not the case. His first memories are located in a realm, or state, of what he called the Earthworm's-Eye View of the world. It was a murky and opaque experience. He had no memory of who he was, or where he was. It was a strange, confusing form of existence: which felt like being "underground" within a murky mysterious environment, with roots or blood vessels running through it. There were also strange sounds and noises, like pounding, and occasionally distorted features of creatures appearing and disappearing inside the mud. Thankfully he did not remain there though. At some point he became aware of a wondrous spinning light, which was also emitting an incredibly beautiful melody. This spinning, gorgeous white light gradually revealed itself to be not only a luminous musical apparition, but also a gateway, a portal, to a very different type of world:

"An opening. I was no longer looking *at* the slowly spinning light at all, but *through* it.

The moment I understood this, I began to move up. Fast. There was a whooshing sound, and in a flash I went through the opening and found myself in a completely new world. The strangest, most beautiful world I'd ever seen.

Brilliant, vibrant, ecstatic, stunning … I could heap on one adjective after another to describe what this world looked and felt like, but they'd short. I felt like I was being born. Not reborn, or born again. Just born.

Below me there was countryside. It was green, lush, and earthlike. It *was* earth ... but at the same time it wasn't. It was like when your parents take you back to a place where you spent some years as a very young child. You don't know the place. Or at least you think you don't. But as you look around, something pulls at you, and you realize that a part of yourself - a part way, deep down - does remember the place after all, and is rejoicing at being back there again.

I was flying, passing over trees and fields, streams and waterfalls, and here and there, people. There were children, too, laughing and playing. ... The word *real* expresses something abstract, and it's frustratingly ineffective at conveying what I'm trying to describe. Imagine being a kid and going to a movie on a summer day. Maybe the movie was good, and you were entertained as you sat through it. But then the show ended, and you filed out of the theater and back into the deep, vibrant, welcoming warmth of the summer afternoon. And as the air and the sunlight hit you, you wondered why on earth you'd wasted this gorgeous day sitting in a dark theater.

Multiply that feeling a thousand times, and you still won't be anywhere close to what it felt like where I was."

- Eben Alexander, ***Proof of Heaven***

The realm was described as similar to Earth at its most bucolic, but also qualitatively different. A phrase is used, which is often attested to by people who have experienced DMT realms, that it was essentially "*more real than real*," that these places possess a "hyperreality" which is more intense and perceptually richer than our ordinary material world. The scenes he witnessed were enthused with a joy and happiness which was palpable and sensual, and he felt himself a "speck of awareness on a butterfly wing," one of many swooping through this lush and lustrous habitat. He also became aware of a companion, who seemed to be caring for him, and accompanying and guiding him through his travels in this startlingly new world. This was the "girl on the butterfly wing" who would later on become one of the most compelling aspects of his adventure. Her personal warmth and presence not only welcomed him into this beautiful world, but she also had another role as well: to introduce him to the Being who lay at the heart of all realms, all dimensions, and all universes. This is the Being he refers to as the "Core." The benevolent entity which was not only the source of everything that exists, but also the source of all consciousness as well. This Being was to communicate to him that he would be "shown many things" but that he would also be "going back." Back to an existence and life he could scarcely remember, and back to a family who were desperately praying for his safe return:

"I continued moving forward and found myself entering an immense void, completely dark, infinite in size, yet also infinitely comforting. Pitch black as it was, it was also brimming with light: a light that seemed to come from a brilliant orb that I now sensed near me. An orb that was living and almost solid, as the songs of the angel beings had been.

My situation was, strangely enough, something akin to that of a fetus in a womb. The fetus floats in the womb with the silent partner of the placenta, which nourishes it and mediates its relationship to the everywhere present yet at the same time invisible mother. In this case, the "mother" was God, the Creator, the Source who is responsible for making the universe and all in it. This Being was so close that there seemed to be no distance at all between God and myself. Yet at the same time, I could sense the infinite vastness of the Creator, could see how completely miniscule I was by comparison. I will occasionally use *Om* as the pronoun for God because I originally used that name in my writings after my coma. "Om" was the sound I remembered hearing associated with that omniscient, omnipotent, and unconditionally loving God, but any descriptive word falls short.

The pure vastness separating Om and me was, I realized, why I had the Orb as my companion. In some manner I couldn't completely comprehend but was sure of nonetheless, the Orb was a kind of "interpreter" between me and this extraordinary presence surrounding me.

It was as if I was being born into a larger world, and the universe itself was like a giant cosmic womb, and the Orb (who remained in some way connected to the Girl on the Butterfly Wing, who in fact *was* she) was guiding me through this process.

Later, when I was back here in the world, I found a quotation by the seventeenth-century Christian poet Henry Vaughan that came close to describing this place - this vast, inky-black core that was the home of the Divine itself.

"There is, some say, in God a deep but dazzling darkness ..."

That was it, exactly: an inky darkness that was also full to brimming with light.

The questions, and the answers, continued. Though they still didn't come in the form of language as we know it, the "voice" of this Being was warm and - odd as I know this may sound - personal. It understood humans, and it possessed the qualities we possess, only in infinitely greater measure. It knew me deeply and overflowed with qualities that all my life I've always associated with human beings, and human beings alone: warmth, compassion, pathos ... even irony and humour.

Through the Orb, Om told me that there is not one universe but many - in fact, more than I could conceive - but that love lay at the center of them all. Evil was present in all the other universes as well, but only in the tiniest trace amounts. Evil was necessary because without it free will was impossible, and without free will there could be no growth - no forward movement, no chance for us to become what God longed for us to be. Horrible and all-powerful as evil sometimes seemed to be in a world like ours, in the larger picture love was overwhelmingly dominant, and it would ultimately be triumphant.

I saw the abundance of life throughout the countless universes, including some whose intelligence was advanced far beyond that of humanity. I saw that there are countless higher dimensions, but that the only way to know these dimensions is to enter and experience them directly. They cannot be known, or understood, from lower dimensional space. Cause and effect exist in these higher realms, but outside of our earthly conception of them. The world of time and space in which we move in this terrestrial realm is tightly and intricately meshed within these higher worlds. In other words, these worlds aren't totally apart from us, because all worlds are part of the same overarching divine Reality. From these higher worlds one could access any time or place in our world.

It will take the rest of my life, and then some, to unpack what I learned up there. The knowledge given me was not "taught" in the way that a history lesson or math theorem would be. Insights happened directly, rather than needing to be coaxed and absorbed. Knowledge was stored without memorization, instantly and for good. It didn't fade, like ordinary information does, and to this day I still possess all of it, much more clearly than I possess the information that I gained over all of my years in school.

That's not to say that I can get this knowledge just like that. Because now that I'm back here in the earthly realm, I have to process it through my limited physical body and brain. But it's there, I feel it, laid into my very being. For a person like me who had spent his whole life working hard to accumulate knowledge and understanding the old-fashioned way, the discovery of this more advanced level of learning was, alone, enough to give me food for thought for ages to come ..."

- Eben Alexander, *Proof of Heaven*

As he became more familiar with the ontology of these different realms, he found it easier to pass through them, but usually accompanied by his guide and companion, who seemed to chaperone him through these tiers. Each time he would be schooled with different insights and intimations of the nature of the universe (or multiverse) and the underlying nature of the reality which forms it. And each time he would find himself back in the Earthworm's-Eye View of the world, and each time the process would begin again. This continued until the Earthly realm was to call him, to implore him, his family and friends who missed him so much, and whose relationship towards him was also driven by probably the most fundamentally important message which the whole experience had given him:

"I found myself wishing for the Spinning Melody to return. After an initial struggle to recall the notes, the gorgeous music, and the spinning ball of light emitting it blossomed into my awareness. They cut, once again, through the jellied muck, and I began to rise.

In the worlds above, I slowly discovered, to know and be able to think of something is all one needs in order to move toward it. To think of the Spinning Melody was to make it appear, and to long for the higher worlds was to bring myself there. The more familiar I became with the world above, the easier it was to return to it. During my time out of body, I accomplished this back-and-forth movement from the muddy darkness of the Realm of the Earthworm's-Eye View to the green brilliance of the Gateway and into the black but holy darkness of the Core any number of times. How many I can't say exactly - again because time as it was there just doesn't translate to our conception of time here on earth. But each time I reached the Core, I went deeper than before, and was taught more, in the wordless, more-than-verbal way that all things are communicated in the worlds above this one.

That doesn't mean that I saw anything like the whole universe, either in my original journey from the Earthworm's-Eye View up to the Core, or in the ones that came afterward. In fact, one of the truths driven home to me in the Core each time I returned to it was how impossible it would be to understand all that exists - either its physical/visible side or its (much, much larger) spiritual/invisible side, not to mention the countless other universes that exist or have ever existed.

But none of that mattered, because I had already been taught the one thing - the only thing - that, in the last analysis, truly matters. I had initially received this piece of knowledge from my lovely companion on the butterfly wing upon my first entrance into the Gateway. It came in three parts, and to take one more shot at putting it into words (because of course it was initially delivered wordlessly), it would run something like this:

You are loved and cherished.
You have nothing to fear.
There is nothing you can do wrong.

If I had to boil this entire message down to one sentence, it would run this way:

You are loved."

- Eben Alexander, ***Proof of Heaven***

At some point, however, within the murky dark realm six faces appeared in the fug, faces he could barely recognise, but were praying for him, in fear and anguish to return to them. He somehow understood primordially that they needed him, that he had responsibilities to them, and that he must return. And return he did, which after a period of natural convalescence he would return to the world with a message of hope and illumination. This is demonstrated by the reception and success of his book, which has now become a global bestseller. Some of his critics have labelled his book "unscientific" and claimed that this was simply a hallucination which was created during the period when the brain "rebooted" as he returned from his coma. Others have claimed that it was a hallucination induced by abnormal quantities of DMT in this critical period (hence the "hyperreality" of the experience). This is an interesting hypothesis, what is quite droll though, is that the most leading researcher in this field (Rick Strassman) who has conducted the only authorised DMT field studies over a number of years, himself believes that the realms encountered under the influence of DMT, may in fact be *authentic*, independent realities in their own right. The DMT hypothesis therefore reinforces the credibility of the story more than it undermines it, though his critics are no doubt unaware of this. Anybody who has witnessed the many interviews and speeches Eben Alexander has given in response to his book, will testify to not only the extensive research he has obviously conducted to scientifically illuminate his experience, but also the obvious warm sincerity of his personality. Qualities no doubt strengthened by the incredible nature of his experience.

What Alexander's story also seems to provide, is not only a striking *ontology* - which seems to corroborate the understanding of consciousness as a nonlocal phenomenon, and thereby support the concept of the *survival* of consciousness outside of the brain. He also appears to provide an insight into the two related, but completely different experiences of two of most powerful endogenous "hallucinogens" in the neurochemistry of the brain: N,N-DMT and 5 MeO DMT.

N,N-DMT seems to provide access to the worlds and dimensions that *parallel* and *interpenetrate* ours - these "higher dimensions" and "alternate realities" which co-exist alongside ours, but which we very rarely get to perceive. Our biological wiring is calibrated it seems to usually only receive one "channel," or "Channel Normal" as Rick Strassman judiciously puts it. Only by raising the levels of DMT within our brain chemistry (either endogenously or exogenously), do we get the chance to perceive these alternate worlds which exist within a vast multiverse, which are always there, but simply *imperceptible* to our normal frequency of consciousness.

5 MeO DMT also alters our brain chemistry, but does not access these "alternate worlds" and "parallel realities" which comprise the vast and *multi-dimensional Metaverse*, but instead attunes our consciousness to experience the "frequency" of the Divine Source of all that exists: This is the "spiritual dimension," a dimension outside of both time and space as we usually conceive of them, but also the heart of all existence: This is the realm of the Being of the *"Infinite Void,"* and the *"Shining Darkness,"* "the *Absolute*," and "the *Metaphysical Source of All Reality*," the *"infinite loving God"* of all religions, regardless of creed and denomination. Is this then "the supersensual *Abyss*" of Jakob Boehme, "the *dazzling darkness*" of Vaughan, the *"Ein Sof"* of the Kabbalists, and the *"Gnostic God"* of Philip K. Dick, as well as the *"Absolute Mind"* of Hegel? If so then this *Divine Being* would appear to be the fundamental *root of all consciousness*, and of all

reality, the *essence* and *core* of who we all are, and thereby, for every one of us, our eventual *destination:*

"This last embodiment of spirit - spirit at once gives its complete and true content the form of self, and thereby realises its notion, and in doing so remains within its own notion - this is *Absolute Knowledge*. It is spirit knowing itself in the form of spirit, it is conceptual comprehensive knowledge through notions. Truth is here not merely *in itself* absolutely identical with certainty; it has also the typical form of certainty of self, or in its existence - i.e. for spirit knowing it - it is in the *form* of knowledge of itself."

- G.W.F. Hegel, **The Phenomenology of Mind**

IX

"The universal consequently is free power. It is itself and it encroaches upon its Other, but not by force: in its Other it is quiescent and at home. It has been called free power, but it might also be called free love or unbounded bliss, for it is an attitude of itself to what is distinct as though it were itself; in this it has returned to itself."

- G. W. F. Hegel, *Science of Logic*

Chapter 9

Appendix:
Guy Debord and the Metaphysics of Marxism:
An Obituary of Guy Debord

"The French version of existentialism, lacking any sense of excess, could not contain Debord. We, however, are witness to an amusing, paradoxical spectacle. On the one hand, Sartre, whose first concern was to write for future generations, and who was propelled step by step into the arms of the contemporary, drowning in an ever-widening sea of current affairs. On the other hand, Debord, who was only interested in current affairs and finds himself condemned to work towards a distant future where he faces a posthumous fame, which - if I know him - leaves him cold..."

- Asger Jorn, 1964

"Mankind has grown shorter by a head, and the greatest head of our time to boot."

- Frederick Engels, *Letter to Sorge, 15th March 1883*

"Time, as Hegel showed, is the *necessary* alienation, the environment where the subject realizes himself by losing himself, where he becomes other in order to become truly himself."

- Guy Debord, *The Society of the Spectacle*

I

There will be a number of our contemporaries who will no doubt identify with Engels' eloquent testimonial to his friend and collaborator, Karl Marx, finding perhaps within his statement a similar sentiment to the current loss of the late Guy Debord. If this should sound to some a rather pretentious exaggeration, it should be borne in mind that even disinterested commentators have been forced to conclude that his passing surely constitutes an "end of an era" in French cultural and political history; a man who was the "epitome of intellectual radicalism"; and therefore to others an even more trenchant significance. The formidable vacuum that has been created by his departure predictably enough displays a number of paradoxical qualities. As though he represented possibly one of the last giants of radical theory, a figure of uncompromising rigour; his stature was always curiously belied by his conspicuous absence from public life, a grave gesture to the historical conditions of modern society, whose essential character he was indisputably the ill-famed adversary. This quite self-consciously cultivated sense of authority was therefore always accompanied by the conspiratorial air of a shadowy enigma:

"We had never been seen to be involved in the affairs, quibbles, and the business of the radical left politicians and the progressive intelligentsia. And now that we can flatter ourselves that we have achieved the most shocking notoriety amongst this riff-raff, we will become even less accessible, we will go even more underground. The more famous our theses become, the more obscure we ourselves will be."

- Debord and Sanguinetti, *The Veritable Split in the International*

II

It is not the purpose of this brief article, however, to attempt to elaborate the various myths that envelop the man, as it shall already be taken for granted that most of its readership are already fairly well acquainted with this particular subject. Those who are less familiar can easily gain access to such material from a number of books which are currently available, and are able to cover this topic in rather more detail. We shall have to confine ourselves to the somewhat more neglected aspect of his lifework: his theoretical legacy. Obviously an article of this nature can make no pretension of comprehensiveness - either in exploring the at times profound subtlety of its "metaphysical" detail, or surveying the entirety of its broad sweep of vision. Instead we shall have to be content with a general survey of its key features.

Though Debord's work has gained fame and is certainly appreciated in certain circles in society, it still often appears far from fully understood. Often critics and commentators would evoke the "chiliastic serenity" and the "crystalline perfection" that characterised his prose; the artistic beauty of its construction, as well as the diamond intensity of its style. Indeed it is precisely this dialectical density that both attracted some while intimidating others, hungry to grasp the underlying meaning of his terminology. "Density" is in fact probably the most fitting description to define his theory, as few writers can compare with Debord for condensing such a wealth of analysis in such a compact and concise manner. Its enduring quality lies precisely in the fact that his books' attraction does not diminish through rereading, but is rather enriched and rewarded, as the full force of his meaning becomes increasingly apparent.

It is now commonplace to note that Debord's *magnum opus*, the notorious **The Society of the Spectacle**, was first published by Buchet-Chastel in 1967; the motive for its timing seems two-fold, both distinct and interrelated. Not only did its appearance coincide with the rising discontent and political radicalisation of this period - which was to culminate in the tumultuous events of May 1968 (a social movement the Situationist International both predicted and participated in: "Where there was fire we brought the petrol.") Its arrival was also obviously to parallel Marx's launch, exactly a century before, of his major theoretical work *Capital: A Critique of Political Economy*, Debord no doubt echoing Hegel's observation:

"... since in all periods of the world a political revolution is sanctioned in men's opinions, when it repeats itself. Thus Napoleon was twice defeated and the Bourbon's twice expelled."

- G. W. F. Hegel, *The Philosophy of History*

A point Marx was caustically to take up (following Engels' prompting) adding his own particular twist at the beginning of *The Eighteenth Brumaire of Louis Bonaparte*. This obviously deliberate act of mimicry and sense of reenactment (a theme that was to feature throughout the entire history of the S.I.) was thereby to serve a number of combined purposes. Firstly no doubt to give a clear sense of identity and orientation to the S.I., firmly establishing it within the trajectory of Western Marxism, and also, more boldly, to help stake its claim that it was the *true* heir of the deformed project of the workers' movement, *as well* as the auto-destruction of modern art.

III

The Society of the Spectacle, like everything else in history, a child of its time. Its excellence therefore is firstly a reflection of the period from which it was composed. After the end of the Second World War, Paris had become the cultural capital of the world - a laboratory of intense artistic and intellectual experimentation, which was to produce a pantheon of new movements, and cultural and political figureheads. This fertility was an obvious sign of the enthusiasm of the age "... where one could so easily pass unnoticed." One of Debord's rare qualities was the curious way he straddled both milieux, in a distinct though removed manner - as the nucleus of a somewhat obscure organisation which combined the many-sided talents of the artistic avant-garde, largely jettisoned by the early Sixties, and a rising tide of theoretical militants. This circumstance was to later play a contributory factor to the "conspiracy of silence" that Debord often seemed to be subjected to, as most of his theoretical rivals were on the whole established academics - usually professors of philosophy: from Althusser to Lefebvre, as well as the exiled school of Critical Theorists (Adorno, Horkheimer, Marcuse, etc.). The only notable exception to this rule was Sartre, whose literary and philosophical reputation dominated the period. The intellectual cross-currents which were to shape this generation was the ascendency and renaissance of two of the most influential thinkers in world history: namely the reigning monarch of classical idealism, G. W. F. Hegel, and his rebellious offspring Karl Marx. And it was a critical encounter between these two "mighty thinkers" that was to forge a whole constellation of position-taking methodological approaches of the era. As Merleau-Ponty was to recognise in one of his influential works:

"All the great philosophical ideas of the past century - the philosophies of Marx and Nietzsche, phenomenology, German existentialism, psychoanalysis - had their beginnings in Hegel"

- Merleau Ponty, **Sense and Non-sense**

In fact, it was another of Merleau-Ponty's works, **Adventures of the Dialectic**, that was to focus attention upon the book which was to provide the key locus and foundation of **The Society of the Spectacle**. That book was an early collection of essays by the Hungarian Marxist philosopher Georg Lukacs, and was named **History and Class Consciousness**. The Fifties and the Sixties were to turn Paris into a theatre of philosophical revisionism, mainly in an attempt to salvage Marxism from what was being considered as the ideological deformation of Stalinism, which after its repudiation at the Twentieth

Congress of the C. P. S. U. was seen as contaminated by atrocity. In a bid to rescue the materialist conception of history, and with it the fate of the workers' movement, intense interest was centred on the history of Marxism - at its genesis and permutations, to discover the origins of its corruption. Here the rediscovery of the philosophical revisionists of the early Twenties was to provide valuable source material for the rethinking of Marxism itself, and this was bolstered by the translation and publication of the early, so called "humanist" works of the young Marx (namely the ***Economic and Philosophical Manuscripts of 1844*** as well as ***The German Ideology***, both unpublished during his lifetime). The main achievement of Lukacs was that he was the first major Marxist thinker, who through his comprehensive knowledge of classical philosophy was to reawaken interest in the birth of historical materialism from its origins in German idealism, reestablishing Hegel as its central precursor. Not only this, he also attempted to resynthesize the whole methodological approaches of the two systems to provide a new basis for a Marxist theory of consciousness. He thereby portrayed Marx as not only the dissenting pupil of the Hegelian dialectical method, having turned it "right-side up" to provide the central framework of materialism: "the science of history" as ***The German Ideology*** was boldly to proclaim, but equally its direct descendent and culmination:

"... our underlying premise here is the belief that in Marx's theory and method the *true method* by which to understand history has *finally* been discovered."

- Georg Lukacs, ***History and Class Consciousness***

IV

This identification of Marxism with the consistent application of Hegelian dialectical method was also later embraced by Debord and heralded as the essence of critical Marxism. Confirmation of this adherence was clearly provided by the lifelong allegiance of not only Marx, but equally Engels (very much a connoisseur of Hegel) to the debt they owed their mentor. This was also true of many of the key figures of their day, often friends and rivals, from Ferdinand Lassalle, to Michael Bakunin, Alexander Herzen to Max Stirner. When later in life, particularly after the first volume of ***Capital,*** a new generation of "system builders" (like the German socialist professor Eugene Duhring) were proclaiming the *Absolute Knowledge* of their theoretical doctrines, pompously denigrating many of the titans of philosophy, like Kant and Hegel, both Marx and Engels were to leap to the defence of their predecessors, lambasting the pretensions of their "pygmy plagiarisers" (see Engels ***Anti-Duhring***). This position was also apparent and made vividly clear in one of Engels' last works, though its mode of exposition, and at times clumsy philosophical conception was to feed into the controversies of another generation:

"... ultimately the Hegelian system merely represents a materialism idealistically turned on its head in method and content."

- Frederick Engels, ***Ludwig Feuerbach and the End of Classical German Philosophy***

To Debord it was precisely the estrangement of Marxism from its roots in the dialectical method which fed in into its degeneration in the hands of the socialist theoreticians of the Second International. Firstly with the intransigence of Kautsky, whose scientific conception of socialism was founded more on a mechanical and evolutionary model of history (borrowed mainly from Darwin). Bernstein's disaffection from the orthodoxy of "scientific socialism" to a complete revisionism, and reformism of Marxism, was to provide the first evidence of the theories breach with reality:

"The inseparability of Marx's theory from the Hegelian method is itself inseparable from the revolutionary character of the theory, namely its truth."

- Guy Debord, *The Society of the Spectacle*

V

Lukacs's position in the early Twenties was also mirrored, and amplified by the contemporaneous work of another pivotal Western Marxist, Karl Korsch, whose unorthodox *Marxism and Philosophy* was published in the same year as *History and Class Consciousness*, and was to share the Comintern's wrath and likewise branded "revisionist." The fact that both Korsch and Lukacs were professors of philosophy was viewed as the obvious source of their Hegelian deviationism and ideological error. This was to to throw in motion a set of events that were to mark both men for the rest of their lives. For Lukacs it was the first of a number of self-criticisms that would tactically secure his affiliation to the now Moscow dominated Communist movement, and also led to his accommodation with Stalinism. For Korsch it was the beginning of his rupture with the Comintern, which would lead to expulsion and exile. In 1923 however, their work was branded together, and recognised as at least *sharing* some key features. In an Afterword to *Marxism and Philosophy* Korsch was to concur:

"As far as I am able to establish, I am in fundamental agreement with the themes of the author (Lukacs) which relate in many ways to the questions raised in this work, if based on a broader philosophical foundation."

While Lukacs had concentrated on founding a new theory of consciousness, Korsch was to apply scrutiny to the history of Marxism itself, and its relation to the totality. To Korsch, theory was the conceptual expression of the real movement of history, in contradistinction to ideology, which was a partial, or congealed apprehension of reality. Using this frame of reference, Korsch was to subject the development and history of Marxism to a dialectical examination. This was to lead him to formulate a periodisation of its development and its relationship to the proletariat, of which it was to be its theoretical expression. The first period lead up to 1848 and the outbreak of the various European revolutions, with Marxism representing an integrated critique which was conceived as a living totality. The second stage was to correspond to the ebbing of the workers' movement, and the years of political reaction throughout Europe in which Marx would devote himself to the study of the fundamental science of capitalist society - political economy. As the science of history became fragmented into a number of different disciplines, with the scientific critique of the economy taking centre-stage, this was seen to rob Marxism of its philosophical dimension, and explain why it had eventually developed and culminated in the positivistic "orthodoxy" of scientism within the Second International:

"We have already mentioned that Marx and Engels themselves always denied that scientific socialism was any longer a philosophy. But it is easy to show irrefutably, by reference to the sources, that what the revolutionary dialecticians Marx and Engels meant by the opposite of philosophy was something very different to what it meant to later vulgar-Marxism. Nothing was further from them than the claims to impartial, pure, theoretical study, above class differences ..."

- Karl Korsch, *Marxism and Philosophy*

The third period of Marxism, at the beginning of this century, was when an attempt was made, in conjunction with reality, to return to revolutionary Marxism (Luxemburg, Lenin, etc.). Here Korsch was to demonstrate that there was a peculiar parallel between scientific socialism's conception of the problems of the state and philosophy, and the means of their suppression and abolition; that the continuation of the state and philosophy as separate spheres was characteristic of the theoreticians of the Second International. A number of these questions were to also preoccupy the imprisoned Communist leader Antonio Gramsci, in the light of his experiences of the councilist movement 1918-20 in Italy. As Debord notes:

"Throughout his life, Marx had maintained a unitary point of view in his theory, but the *exposition* of the theory was carried out on the *terrain* of the dominant thought and became precise in the form of critiques of particular disciplines, principally the critique of the fundamental science of capitalist society, political economy. It is this mutilation, later accepted as definitive, which has constituted "Marxism.""

- Guy Debord, ***The Society of the Spectacle***

Debord was highly influenced by this approach, and its traces are deeply embedded within ***The Society of the Spectacle***'s arguably most famous chapter: "*The Proletariat as Subject and as Representation.*" Not only was Debord to take up this mode of analysis, he also went on to not only uncover the degeneracy of European reformism, but equally its complementary parallel: Marxist-Leninism. Most of the philosophical revisionists were essentially sympathetic to Lenin, and his stature was based on him having combated many of the strains of European reformism, and reestablishing the principal features of revolutionary Marxism. Only later was Korsch to make a frontal attack on Lenin's tactics and conceptions (moving to a similar position as Pannekoek). The key source of Lenin's authoritarianism was viewed as a product of Russian backwardness, and the particularly hostile political conditions in which the Bolshevik Party was forced to operate. Its prestige after the October Revolution was to reverberate throughout the world Communist movement, as its ideological orthodoxy as well as political policy came to dominate party affairs internationally. The disastrous course of Russian history, which was to evolve into the terroristic totalitarianism of Stalin, was later viewed as an outcome whose seeds lay in the authoritarian elitism of the Bolsheviks as formed by Lenin, as the party apparatus germinated into a monolithic bureaucracy after seizing control of the state. The key organisational lessons which Debord was to draw from this monstrous miscarriage of Leninism, was chiefly acquired from the works of the philosophical revisionists, who were essentially most favourable to the practice of *council communism* as the true model of proletarian revolution, in which theory and practice could be met in conditions that would be adequate to each other. When Debord was to develop and reformulate the current stage and conditions of class struggle in modern society - and with it the central goal of *autogestion* (or complete and generalised self-management), he was to identify the means of this struggle through the formation of *workers' councils*.

VI

We now move on to the equally fertile critique of the contemporary features of modern society and the historical force which drives it: *advanced capitalism*. Throughout the Fifties and Sixties the Situationists were to launch their attack on the nature of modern consumer capitalism, and undertake a searing judgement on modern life. Debord was to adopt much of the critique of Lukacs as the underlying premise of contemporary *alienation* - as originally elaborated in **History and Class Consciousness**, the centrepiece of which is the classic essay "*Reification and the Consciousness of the Proletariat.*" `Here Lukacs was to explore the consequences of the social relations of modern capitalism based on the commodity structure of society, grounded mainly on Marx's analysis of "commodity fetishism" in **Capital**. Here Lukacs was skilfully to utilise his knowledge of classical philosophy, in particular German idealism, as a backdrop for investigating capitalism's effect upon man's social consciousness. Although commodity exchange existed in primitive societies, it was only a marginal activity and therefore only had a corresponding social impact. As capitalism developed however, the commodity form became dominant and structured their lives accordingly. In this environment in which the commodity based society develops, and takes on a greater complexity, this social relation is progressively hidden as a "veil of mystification" descends on its participants; and social relations between people become transformed into relations between "things." The world of things ruled men through objective laws which were independent of them. The general results of this "reification" is the increasing rationalisation of society, and with it a general atomisation in which the intrinsic interconnection of things is gradually eroded and lost:

"Just as the capitalist system continually produces and reproduces itself economically on higher and higher levels, the structure of reification progressively sinks deeper, more fatefully and more definitively into the consciousness of man."

- Georg Lukacs, ***History and Class Consciousness***

Debord was to adopt this course of analysis as the foundation of his critique of modern consumer capitalism, in which alienated labour was not liberated by the expanding terrain of consumption, but rather complemented and reinforced by it. The rise of consumer society was not then a qualitative break from the economy of production, but simply its extension, as the underlying laws that governed each of these areas were essentially the same. Despite the material enrichment that accompanies the mass production of commodities, this development can in fact be no more than an expansion of *survival*, leaving the quality of life (the conditions of production) untouched. In fact the greater the extent of the conquest of the commodity, the more estranged, the more removed will people be from their own existences:

"The spectacle in society corresponds to a concrete manufacture of alienation. Economic expansion is mainly the expansion of this specific industrial production. What grows with the economy in-motion-for-itself can only be the very alienation which was at its origin."

- Guy Debord, *The Society of the Spectacle*

VII

On this premise Debord was to found his critique of all aspects of life in modern consumer society, in a quest to identify clearly the galloping unreality of modern life: the pseudo-quality, boredom, and banality which seem to be such an integral feature of the contemporary world. The decline and decomposition of everyday life was viewed as resulting from its colonisation by the commodity - where the gratification of human needs were being continuously reproduced by the avarice of commodity logic. The subsequent dehumanisation of modern life was therefore only a *consequence* of the consumer onslaught itself. In this environment, where consumption is the *ultimate goal* of social life, all human relations become tailored to this model, and life becomes a lurid parade in which all merchandise battle for recognition with their increasing claims of total satisfaction. This tendency was also to find its *nec plus ultra* with the corresponding rise of information technology, a medium whose very form seemed to exemplify its social content. As the mass production of commodities spread across the surface of society, it was equally paralleled and reinforced by the emergence of mass communication, which would help facilitate its advance. The media surge through this unilateral system of communication was to form the kernel of Debord's conceptual tool for analysing these social mechanisms. That concept was of course *spectacle*. The term was to denote both a general and a particular form. Generally it was viewed as the whole social process where man's production of his overall environment had become transformed into tools for the creation of separations. Specifically it was to define an inversion, or rupture, within reality which was created by a spectacular society. This rupture was actually the outcome of the feature of independent *representation*, and its disjunction of the totality; the dialectical interaction of thought and practice: "the image has become the final form of commodity reification." This disjunction had created a cleavage in reality in which an inversion was constituted:

"Reality considered *partially* unfolds, in its own general unity, as a pseudo-world *apart*, an object of mere contemplation. The specialisation of images of the world is completed in the world of the autonomous image, where the liar has lied to himself."

- Guy Debord, **The Society of the Spectacle**

Though it is worth remembering that what is principally being defined is *not* the medium itself *in the abstract*, so much as the social relation it embodies. It would at this point be helpful to recognise that much of the terminology and mode of analysis, the concepts employed and their mediating interrelationship, stems from Hegelian dialectical methodology. In fact the whole book itself is saturated with (Marxist) Hegelianism. The overall structure of the book is actually borrowed from the **Lesser Logic** of the **Encyclopedia of Philosophical Sciences**, which is a condensed version of the monumental **Science of Logic**. The **Science of Logic**, the "Bible of Hegelianism" is in fact the centrepiece of Hegel's momentous system of absolute idealism, and was to demonstrate the whole ontological structure of reality, or *"Absolute"* as Hegel defined it. It is a very abstruse work - pure metaphysics - and the dialectical nature of reality portrayed in pure naked form. Although it is a notoriously difficult work to master, trying to scale its fatiguing as well as dizzying heights, it can only be counselled that those who are able to complete the journey are certainly in a position to perceive Debord more clearly. Though formally discredited as an ontological exposition of absolute idealism, it still continues to inspire many Marxists. As it represents a complete "veiled" formulation of dialectical materialism, so fluency with it is indispensable for a full comprehension of Marxism:

"It is impossible completely to understand Marx's ***Capital*** and especially its first chapter without having thoroughly studied and understood the *whole* of Hegel's ***Logic***. Consequently, half a century later none of the Marxists understood Marx!!"

- V. I. Lenin, ***Philosophical Notebooks***

VIII

The Hegelian dimension of Debord is also conspicuously present in one of the most neglected features of ***The Society of the Spectacle***, which is in fact its very marrow. And that is the central chapters on time and history. Here Debord was to give free reign to one of his central preoccupations, and to provide us with one of his most original contributions to historical materialism - the relationship of man and time. In his last film he was to draw attention to this aspect of his work in a very blunt fashion:

"The sensation of time slipping has always been a key one for me, and I have been attracted to it, just as others are attracted to the void or water."

- Guy Debord, ***In Girum Imus Nocte et Consumimur Igni***

The key chapter "*Time and History*" begins with probably one of the most potent allegories of the Hegelian notion of unfolding totality. This allegory is given by way of an illustration, a graphic and resonant image, although it's a somewhat opaque contribution to the contentious debate concerning the dialectic of nature:

"History is a real part of *natural history*, of the transformation of nature into man" (Marx). Inversely, this "natural history" has no existence other than through the process of human history, the only part which captures the historical totality, like the modern telescope whose sight captures, *in time*, the retreat of nebulae at the periphery of the universe. History has always existed, but not always in a historical form."

- Guy Debord, ***The Society of the Spectacle***

The genesis and development of human history is then chronicled and portrayed in a manner which is an unorthodox, yet compatible, perspective on the typical Marxist perception of historical materialism. Classical Marxism is essentially rooted in man's economic development, and the forces and relations of production, through the development of society through its progressive interaction and control of nature. This process is usually conceived in the basic paradigm of the base and superstructure metaphor. That upon the economic base of society man erects a social superstructure (political, religious, ideological, etc.) which is in essential correspondence with the current stage of economic development: "It is not the consciousness of men which determines their existence: it is rather their social existence which determines their consciousness." To complement this model, Debord stresses another component of man's ideological formation, which is the conception and social relation with time (the early model of cyclical time which was rooted in the seasonal features of agricultural based societies; the birth of the first monotheistic religions as the first hybrid conception of irreversible time, etc.) What this chapter visibly displays is also clear traces of the Hegelian odyssey of history, of man's journey to self-consciousness through its course. It is therefore the heir not only to the encyclopedic ***The Philosophy of History***, but equally, and even more distinctly, ***The Phenomenology of Mind***. In Engels' later writing he was summoned to recall and elaborate Marxism's relationship to classical philosophy, and how one of its keys to unlocking the "riddle of history" was provided by the ***Phenomenology***:

"... which one may call a parallel to the embryology or paleontology of the mind, an evolution of the individual consciousness through its different stages, expressed in the form of an abbreviated reproduction of the stages through which the consciousness of man has passed in the course of history"

> - Frederick Engels, ***Ludwig Feuerbach and the End of Classical German Philosophy***

This course was to lead us right to the heart of modern society, and its portrayal in the chapter *"Spectacular Time."* The current model and measurement of social time was that of commodity production, the current unit of rationalised labour-power - the quantified unit of commodity time. Here Debord has established that a part of capitalism's intrinsic functioning was founded upon the present social organisation of time, and determined that one of the key features of the present "paralysis of history" was rooted within the ossified congealment of time, of its abstract equivalence (see also Marx's ***The Poverty of Philosophy***).

Limitations of space bar the possibility of any real consideration of the subsequent three chapters, which are devoted to the subjects of urbanism, culture, and psychology respectively. All three chapters are striking in their content, clearly displaying the Situationists intense preoccupation with the questions of modern art and the urban environment. The final chapter is most distinctive with its utilisation of the concepts of Joseph Gabel, a Marxist clinical psychologist who was highly influenced by the "Lukacs Question," and attempted to extend Lukacs theories of consciousness, and apply them to the study of mental pathology.

IX

The Society of the Spectacle has now passed into one of the most peculiar categories in literature: it has become an obscure classic. Its status has always been a strange product of its history, and has largely remained outside of academic canonisation, although it is increasingly being moved within the ambit of mainstream and established publishers. As historically not only has its theme telescoped with time, but equally its pertinence will always be recalled against the backdrop of the events of May 1968.

In 1988 Debord was to extend the work with his only other major theoretical text: ***Comments on the Society of the Spectacle***. Yet again Debord was to demonstrate his particular talent, or even art, of sketching the broad features of an epoch through his skilful though sweeping brushwork. The style remains the same, but the tone has changed. Gone is the totalising Lukacsianism that characterised his earlier work, on the conjunction of theory and history, in which not only did thought seek its realisation in practice, but equally practice found theory. The gravity of the message is as ever only subdued by the elegance of the style. Debord thereby recounts the fundamental movements of his times. His countenance is now more that of a classical historian recording for posterity the notable events unfolding within his epoch: "... thus ended the second year of the war of which Thucydides has written the history." Not only has the spectacle recovered from the assaults that shook its foundations in the late Sixties, now it has advanced, and through chemical combination of its two complementary forms, diffused and concentrated, merged to form a strengthened *integrated* spectacle. Though the message is grave, it is not fatalistic - though the impervious advance of modern capitalism has transformed the world so completely that for the bulk of society the only conventions one is familiar with are its own. It has raised a generation which conforms to its laws. This is not meant in the narrow ideological sense, but rather the seductive and mutating phantasmagoria of the media landscape. Alongside these developments is of course the decades of political reaction which have dominated world politics, and which serves as a barometer to spectacular society. Whether its health is now immutable, however, still remains in the realm of uncertainty. With these two works Debord has surely immortalised himself. To recall the words of Engels once more, this time at the burial of his recently deceased friend and colleague: "His name will live on through the centuries, and so will his work." The question as to who will be able to advance this inheritance is as yet still to be resolved, though in concluding it will be advised to recall the message of the man who was to influence Debord deeply:

"This account of the genesis and aim of these essays is offered less as an apology than a stimulus - and this is the true aim of the work - to make the problem of dialectical method the focus of a discussion as an urgent living problem. If these essays provide the beginning or even just the occasion for a genuinely profitable discussion of dialectical method, if they succeed in making dialectics generally known again, then they will have fulfilled their function perfectly."

- Georg Lukacs, **History and Class Consciousness**
(Steven Turner, *January - February, 1995*)

"Yet whenever I go out on the streets my being somehow reels back appalled: these terrible faces, these machines, they are me too, I know that's not my fault. Everyone's life is a switch between changing oneself and changing the world. Surely they must somehow be the same thing and a dynamic balance is possible. I think the S.I. had this for a while, and later they lost it. I want to find it again - that quickening in oneself and in others, that sudden happiness and beauty. It could connect, it could come together. Psychoanalysis and Trotskyists are both silly old men to the child. Real life is elsewhere."

- Christopher Gray, **Leaving the Twentieth Century**
The Incomplete Work of the Situationist International

"I stood there transfixed. The drizzle was falling on the wooden fence surrounding the yard, on the washing line bare apart from a few clothespins, and on the roof of the garage next door. This was Terrible Beauty, again - but this time far more terrible than ever before.

The world was transfigured, and I was looking into the Godhead.

All the strength had drained from my body, and I just stood there in the rain. I thought I was going to cry, or black out. For this was all I ever wanted: to know that this world and the holy were one and the same: to know that we are not abandoned, nor have we ever been. Nor, so far as I could see standing there that dawn in the rain, was it possible that we ever could be."

- Christopher Gray, ***The Acid Diaries***
A Psychonaut's Guide to the History and Use of LSD

Printed in Great Britain
by Amazon.co.uk, Ltd.,
Marston Gate.